Orphans and Infants
of
Prince George's County
Maryland

1696-1750

Dorothy H. Smith

HERITAGE BOOKS
2011

HERITAGE BOOKS

AN IMPRINT OF HERITAGE BOOKS, INC.

Books, CDs, and more—Worldwide

For our listing of thousands of titles see our website
at
www.HeritageBooks.com

Published 2011 by
HERITAGE BOOKS, INC.
Publishing Division
100 Railroad Ave. #104
Westminster, Maryland 21157

International Standard Book Numbers
Paperbound: 978-1-58549-536-8
Clothbound: 978-0-7884-8804-7

To My Family
June 7, 1976

PREFACE

Rent Rolls, Debt Books and Land Records are important to the Genealogical Record Searcher in establishing the residence of our forebears. The Probate Records may show planning for the distribution of their worldly goods, however, the Court Records yield information that may be helpful in creating a picture of the young American and the 'courses' he travelled in life either by direction of a parent or a guardian, or by the Court.

In September 1663 the Upper House indicated a necessity for including the words (Handy craft, Trade) in the Additional Act for the advancement of Childrens Estates[1]. A male Orphan could receive his Estate at age 21, and a female Orphan at 16 or day of marriage[2]. Servants transported out of Virginia were to complete the time of Servitude here as they ought to have served there and no more. Owners of such servants, claiming more than five years of Servitude were to bring them into the County Court, within Six months after receiving them into their custody and the Court adjudged their Ages, and the same was recorded[3]. Freedom dues consisted mainly of clothing and in addition to the clothing the men were to receive "2 hoes, 1 axe and 1 gun of 20 shillings price, not above four foot by the barrel, nor less than three and an half", and the females were to receive "three barrels of Indian corn" in addition to the clothing[4]. Rules of the Court were amended from time to time, however, I believe some of the Laws presented here may be helpful in understanding Court Procedures in the early 18th Century.

I wish to thank the Hall of Records of Maryland for Authorization to reproduce Prince George's County Court Proceedings, 1696-1750 for publication in Orphans and Infants of Prince George's County, Maryland 1696-1750.

The Compiler

1. William Hand Browne, editor, Archives of Maryland, Volume I. Proceedings and Acts of the General Assembly of Maryland- January 1637/8 to September 1664. Baltimore: Maryland Historical Society, 1883, p. 470.
2. Acts of 1715, Chapter 39, sections 13 and 15 in Thomas Bacon, Laws of Maryland. Annapolis: Jonas Green, Printer to the Province, 1765
3. Ibid., Chapter 44, Sections 14 and 15.
4. Ibid., Chapter 44, Section 10.

FOREWORD

In preparing this record, the Indices of over twenty volumes of the County Court Proceedings of Prince Georges County, Maryland from 1696 through 1750 were scanned at the Hall of Records in Annapolis, Maryland. Where the word 'bound', 'adjudged', or 'age' appeared after a name, the information was recorded. In most instances the record is complete as recorded. However, in some cases only basic information was abstracted, such as age, name of parents and/or to whom bound. The Court Session appears in the left hand margin. Beneath the Court Session, the Liber and Folio in which the information was recorded is cited. The names of the orphans or infants are recorded in alphabetical order. An index has been prepared of the parents and guardians.

Dorothy H. Smith
(Mrs. Marlin R. Smith, Sr.)

Dorothy H. Smith
1924 Old Annapolis Blvd.
Annapolis, Maryland 21401

ORPHANS AND INFANTS OF PRINCE GEORGES COUNTY, MARYLAND
1696-1750

August 1747
GG 90

AARON, Moses an Infant born the tenth day
of June last is by the Court here bound unto
John Winn Senr. untill he Arrives to the Age
of Twenty-one years and the said John Winn
Senr is by the same Court allowed Fifteen
hundred pounds of Tobacco for the Trouble
& Expence which he has allready sustained
in keeping & maintaining the said Infant.

November 1727
N 613

ABBESS, Mary six months old the last day of
this Month November Instant is by the Court
here bound unto William Clark till she arrives to the age of Sixteen years & in respect of it's infancy the said William Clarke
is allowed in the present Levy nine hundred
pounds of Tobacco, whereupon he promises in
open Court here to learn the said Mary during the time af'd to read distinctly in the
bible & at the expiration thereof to give
her a Decent Suit of apparel-

March 1746
DD 410

ABINGTON, Bowles is by the Court here admitted to Choose his Guardian and thereupon he makes Choice of John Needham of
Prince Georges County Gentleman who in his
proper person in Court here declares his
Willingness to accept the Same. Whereupon
the Court orders that Doctor Andrew Scott
Deliver unto John Needham the Present

Guardian all the Estate or felial Portion
of the aforesaid Bowles Abington which the
said John Needham is required to take Possession of and thereupon at the next County
Court to give Sufficient Security agreeable
to the Law in that Case made and Provided.

March 1746
DD 410

ABINGTON, John is by the Court here admitted
to Choose his Guardian and thereupon he makes
Choice of John Needham of Prince Georges
County Gentleman who in his proper person
in Court here declares his Willingness to
accept the same.

March 1715
G 719

ACTON, Aron being brought into open Court was
bound to Robert Lloyd and his Assigns till
he attaine ye Age of Twenty One years, being
four Years old next August.

March 1750
LL 134

ANDERSON, Mary Aged about Two years the fifth
Day of February Last by the Court Bound unto
Humphry Whitmore Untill She Arrive to the
Age of Sixteen years. Agreement:-A Years
Schooling and the Customary Freedom Dues at
the Expiration of her Time of Servitude.

June 1720
H 1015

ANDERSON, William Son of Jane Anderson is
by Consent of the Court bound to Jeremiah
Perdue or his assigns till he attains the
age of Twenty one years he being now Thirteen months old.

November 1747
GG 281

ANDREWS, George about two years in August
last is by the Court here bound to Charles
Higginbotham & Margaret his wife untill
Twenty one years. Agreement:- to learn or
Cause the said Orphan to be Learn'd to read
and at the Expiration of the time to give
him the customary Freedom dues.

June 1696
A 11

ASHBY, Marther daughter of Stephen Ashby,
aged 3 yeares or thereabouts bound to
Robert Biggs.

June 1696
A 11

ASHBY, Mary daughter of Stephen Ashby 6
years or thereabouts bound out to William
Conley according to Act of Assembly.

June 1730
P 402

AYRE, James five years old the first day of
June instant is by the Court here bound
unto Allen Lock & Mary his wife until he
the said Minor shall arrive to the age of
twenty one years. Agreement:-to use his
utmost endeavors to learn the said James
to read & write during the term & at the
Expiration thereof to give him a decent
Suit of Apparell.

August 1750   BADEN, John:-aged Seventeen years the ninth
LL 199   Day of December, past AND
              BADEN, Margaret:-aged Fifteen years The last
              Day of July past makes Choice of Thomas Baden
              for their Guardian, Who in his Proper person
              in Court accepts The Same.

November 1720 BARNETT, Elizabeth:-eight years old or there-
K 12   abouts is by the Court here bound unto Gust-
               avus Hesselius untill she arrive to age,
               Whereupon he oblidges himselfe to learn her
               to read and at the expiration of her time
               to give her a Decent Suite of apparell.

August 1703   BARNETT, Luke:- (and Mary Miles) orphant
B 251   children of Thomas Barnett Lately Deceased.
              Nathaniell Wickham & Samuell Brasheer,
              Planters of Prince Georges stand justly in-
              debted...in the full & just Sume of 22 pds-
              8 pence Sterling   26 July 1703

March 1721   BARRACLIFT, John:- Mary Barraclift binds her
K 82   Son John Barraclift being about Eight months
              old unto Thomas Nicholls untill the Said
              Child arrive to the age of Twenty one years,
              Whereupon the said Thomas oblidges himselfe
              to give the said Infant a years schooling.

November 1722 BARRETT, Edward:- is by ye Court here bound
K 650   unto Thos. Bennett & his wife Mary on ye
               Petn of ye sd Tho untill he Comes to age
               being now three years old ye Twentieth of
               January next.

November 1732 BAXTER, George:-aged as tis said in Court
S 117   here Twelve years the twenty-fifth of Nov-
               ember instant is by the Justices thereof
               bound to George Wells until he the said
               George Baxter arrive to the age of Twenty

one years and the said George Wells in his
proper person in Court here Obliges himself
to Learn the said George Baxter to read during his time of Servitude and at the Expiration thereof to give him a Decent Suit of
Apparel.

June 1723
L 82

BEALL,-----:- Elizabeth Bradent by her petition sets forth that a certain woman named
Hannah Beall (whose husband Mathew Beall
dyed some time before) came to her house the
28 day of November last with a young child
& fell sick and so continued till the 8th
day of Aprill following at which time she
the said Hannah dyed---since her death she
has kept her child. Petr. Elizabeth Bradent
allowed 900 pds of Tobacco in the next County
Levy for her trouble and charge above mentioned
and in consideration of her keeping the above
said Child untill next November Court-

November 1725
L 509

BEALL, James:- son of James Beall decd aged
(as 'tis said) 15 years next January comes
into Court here in his proper person and on
his prayer is allowed by the Court here to
Choose his Guardian whereupon he makes choices
of his Mother Sarah Beall and his cousin John
Beall Senr. both of the County afd and they the
afd Sarah and John in their proper persons in
Court here declaring their willingness to
undertake the guardianship of the said James
Beall are by the Justices of the Court here
admitted thereunto-

March 1745
DD 20

BEALL, John:- Son of John is by the Court here
Admitted to Choose his Guardian and hereupon
he makes Choice of Samuell Beall, Junr.

of Prince Georges County Planter who in his
Proper person in Court here declares his
willingness to Accept the Same.

August 1735
V 542

BEALL, Joseph:-Aged as it is said in Court
here Sixteen Years or there abouts is by the
Court here Admitted to choose his Guardian
Whereupon he makes Choice of Thomas Odell of
Prince Georges County Planter who in his
Proper Person in Court here Declares his Will-
ingness to accept the same.

August 1725
L 486

BEALL, Nathaniel:-(of a competent age as tis
said) comes into Court here in his proper
person & on his petition is allowed by ye
Court here to Choose his Guardian whereupon
he makes choice of William Beall Sr. of ye
County afd-and ye sd William in Court agrees.

March 1735
V 350

BEALL, Robert:-Aged as it is Said in Court
here Nineteen Years the Twenty Ninth Day of
next November is by the Court here Admitted
to Choose his guardian Whereupon he Makes
Choice of Thomas Odell of Prince Georges
County Planter who in his proper person in
Court here Declares his Willingness to accept
the same.

November 1725
L 509,510

BEALL, Sarah:-Daughter of James Beall decd
aged (as 'tis said) 13 yeares next April
comes into Court here in her proper person
and on her Prayer is allowed by the Court
here to choose her Guardian whereupon she
makes choice of her Mother Sarah Beall of
the County afsd.-and she the said Sarah the
Mother in her proper person in Court here declaring her willingness to undertake the
guardianship of the said Sarah the Daughter

is by the Justices of the Court here admitted thereunto.

March 1708 BEAMAN, John:-base borne childe of Lidia
C 201   Beaman bound to Tho Blandford untill he
           arrive to ye Age of one and Twenty. The
           said John was borne ye 29th day of Sept.
           Last.

November 1713 BEAUMONT, Darby:-Son of Lidia Beaumont Comes
G 455   into Open Court and is bound by Consent of
               the Court to John Delahunt until he Attaine
               the Age of One and Twenty Yeare's-being three
               Years of Age the first day of June last.

March 1716 BEAUMONT, Darby:-with Approbation of the Court
H 32   is bound unto Murphy Ward and Wife and their
            Assignes till he attain the Age of Twenty-one
            yeares he being six yeares of Age the first
            Day of July next the said Murphy Ward & wife
            or their Assignes to Learn the said Darby
            Beaumont to read and at the Expiration of
            the aforesaid time to give him a New Suit of
            cloaths either Kersey or Drugett two Shirts
            a hatt and a pair of Shoes and Stockins.

June 1748 BECKWITH, Sarah:-an Orphan is by the Court
HH 165   here bound to Hooper Gwynn til she arrives to
           the Age of Sixteen Years and the said Hooper
           Gwynn on his part promises and obliges himself
           to Learn or cause the said Sarah to be Learn'd
           to read and write and to sew Spin & knit and
           at the Expiration of her time of Servitude to
           give her freedom dues according to the Custom
           of the Country.

March 1701 BEEDLE, Mary:-a child of William Beedle Servant
B 99   to Mr. Marsham adjudged to be seven years of
            age. Ordered she Serve according to Law.

March 1717 H 181	BENNETT, Ann:-being Tenn Years old this Day BENNETT, John:-being fourteen Years old next October BENNETT, Sarah:-being Eight Years old next August BENNETT, Thomas:-being Twelve Years Old the Twenty-fifth of December next...All Sons and Daughters of John and Ann Bennett Deceased are bound by consent of the Court to Thomas Bennett and Mary his Wife till they Severally Attain their ages according to Act of Assembly
March 1708 C 209a	BENNETT, Thomas:-an Orphant aged 14 years of age ye 25th day of Aprill next came into Court and bound himselfe to Francis Casteel untill he arrive to ye Age of one and twenty years.
August 1727 N 489	BENTON, Joseph:-(son of Joseph & Anne Benton) two years old the fifteenth day of next October is by the Justices of the Court here bound to Charles Roberts present here in Court in his proper (blank) until it arrive to the age of twenty one years & the said Charles engages to learn the said Child during the time af'd to read distinctly & at the expiration there- of to give him a decent Suit of apparel.
June 1717 H 241	BERRY, Elinor:-is by Consent of the Court bound to John Michael Leverett and Catherine his Wife till She attain her Age according to Act of Assembly being Seven Years and an half Old they to learn her to read in the Bible.
August 1703 B 250,251	BEVEN, Charles: BEVEN, Elizabeth: BEVEN, Kathrine: Mary Beven & Richard Marsham of Prince Georges County indebted unto Charles, Elizabeth and Kathrine Beven, orphant (sic) children unto Charles Beven Lately Deceased.

November 1728
O 331

BIRDWHISTLE, Thomas:-aged two years the twenty second of March next is by the Court here bound to Stephen Hampton until it arrive to Age and the said Stephen in his proper person in Court here promises to learn the said Thomas to read during the term afsd and at the Expiration thereof to give him a decent suit of apparell provided nevertheless that if John Birdwhistle the father of the said Children (see Anne Ray) shall return to these parts and make Satisfaction to the said Stephen for the time he shall keep them that then they the said Anne and Thomas shall be discharged of the above binding-

November 1721
K 421

BIRMINGHAM, Alice:- Eliza Birmingham in Court here binds her Daughter Alice Birmingham unto Mary, the Wife of Daniel Delozer untill it comes to age and the said Daniel in respect of it's Infancy is allowed five hundred pounds of Tobacco in this Levy-

August 1723
L 132

BLACKBURN, Lucy:- is by the Court here bound to Richard Jones untill she arrive to the age of 16 years and he in respect of the Childs Infancy & having maintained her hitherto is allowed 1000 pds of Tobacco in the next Levy to be assest in this County-

November 1727
N 611

BLAKE, Archibald:-born the twenty Second day of April anno Dm Seventeen hundred & twenty one of the consent of his Mother Anne Catherine Blake present here in Court is by the Court here Bound to James Holmeard & his wife until he the said Archibald arrive to the age of twenty one years, hereupon the said James present here in Court in his proper person

obliges himself to Learn the said Minor to
read & write & at the Expiration of the said
time to give him a decent Suit of Apparel.

November 1742   BLAKE, John:-Ordered by the Court here that
AA 192   John Blake aged about Six Years be Bound to
                Thomas Molton until he arrives to the Age of
                Twenty one Years and the said Thomas Molton
                in his proper person in Court here promises
                to Give the said John Blake Two years School-
                ing and at the Expiration of his Time a Decent
                Suit of Apparel.

November 1698   BLANDIGAN, David:-Servant to Mr. John Smith
A 355   adjudged to be 13 years old...to Serve ac-
                cording to Act of Assembly.

June 1711   BLANEY, John:-Sonn of Thomas Blany Deceased
G 69   a year old Last Jan^{ry} bound to Mr. John
                Wright till Age he obleidgeing himself to
                Cause the said Childe to Read.

November 1715   (blank), Sarah:-by Consent of her Mother
H 6   Eliza Rawdry is bound to Mr. Frederick
                Clodius and his wife till she attaine her Age.

June 1711   BLANY, Eliz:-Daughter to Tho. Blany Deceased
G 69   four years of Age ye 2d day of October next
                bound to Mr. James Hadduck till age.

November 1714   BOLTON, James:-by Consent of the Court is
G 692   bound to Paul Rawlins untill he attaine his
                age according to Act of Assembly he being
                Thirteene years of age the Seaventeenth day
                of next Aprill.

June 1748   BOND, James:-Roger Moodie brings into Court
HH 185   a Vagrant boy named James Bond whereupon
                the Court Desires Richard Keene and John
                Cooke Gentlemen to Contract & agree with some
                Master or Commander of a Ship to take the said

James as an Apprentice to make the best
Agreement for the said James's Advantage
'til which time Mr. Benjamin Berry volun-
tarily agrees to take care of and support
the said James Bond.

June 1720
H 1015

BONNER, James:-is by Consent of the Court
bound to David Evans or his Assignes till
he attaine the age of Twenty-one yeares,
the said James Bonner being fifteen months
old.

June 1729
P 2

BOOTHE, John:-aged (as tis said) Eleven Years
next October present here in Court in his
proper person is by the Justices thereof
bound to James Offutt until he the said John
shall arrive to age whereupon the said James
present also in Court here promises to Learn
the said John (during the Term afd) to read
and write and at the Expiration of his Time
to give him a decent Suit of Apparell.

August 1714
G 632

BOOZEMAN, Anne:-by Consent of her Father
Joseph Boozeman is bound to Edward Holmes
and his heires till she attaine her Age
according to Law. She being 4 years old the
the Twenty-fifth day of September next.

August 1714
G 632

BOOZEMAN, William:-by consent of his Father
Joseph Boozeman is bound to Edward Holmes
and his heires till he attaine his Age according to Act of Assembly he being four
years old the Twenty Seaventh of March last.

November 1725
L 550

BOTELER, Alice: BOTELER, Catherine: BOTELER,
Charles: BOTELER, Edward: BOTELER, Henry:
BOTELER, Thomas.--Richard Nermansett of
Prince Georges County, Gent. & Thomas Lin-
gen of Calvert County, Gent. Bond. Richard

Nermansett to pay unto orphans their re-
spective parts or portions of their deceased Fathers Estate-

June 1727
N 351

BOTELER, Thomas:- (Son of Mr. Henry Boteler
deceased) of about Seventeen years of age
(as tis said) comes into Court here & on
his prayer is allowed by the Justices here
to choose his Guardian whereupon he makes
choice of Capt. John Middleton & the said
John Middleton in his proper person in Court
here declaring his willingness to undertake
the Guardianship of the said Thomas is by
the Court here admitted thereunto-

November 1747
GG 292

BOWIE, Eleanor:-BOWIE, Lucy:-BOWIE, Martha:-
Thomas Bowie is by the Court here appointed
Guardian of the Orphans of James Bowie namely
Lucy, Martha and Eleanor and the said Thomas
Bowie in his proper person in Court here
Accepts thereof-

November 1706
C 95a

BOWMAN, Absolon:-an Orphant formerly In Ann
arrundell County bound to Nicholas Roads, now
assigned to Mr. John Garrard he being there
unto Eleven years of Age ye 25 day of March
next. Ordered he Serve ye Said Mr. Garrard
till ye age of one and twenty-

June 1736
W 53

BOYDE, Mary:-aged 11 months & an half this
day to wit the 23 day of June in the 22 year
of his Ldp. the Lord Propry is by the Court
here bound unto Henry Medcalfe until she arrive to age...agreement, to Learn the sd Mary
during the term afd to Read & Write & at the
Expiration thereof to give her a decent Suit
of Apparell-

June 1700

BRADFOARD,------:-Rebecca Shaw comes into Court

B 53 & Bindes her Son, ye sone of Wm. Bradfoard aged 4 years old Last March to Samuell Taylor untill he arrive to the age of one & 20 years.

June 1711
G 69a
BRADLEY, Sarah:- an Orphant neither father nor Mother Liveing five years of age next march bound to Arther Nelson till age he obleidging himselfe to use his Endevour to Cause ye Said Childe to read & Sow and ordered to Serve accordingly.

January 1705
C 35
BRAY, Elizabeth:-Daughter of James Bray an Orphant Nine years of Age bound to Thomas Gibbings till Age.

March 1733
S 246
BROMFIELD, John:-an Orphan Aged as tis said in Court here Thirteen Years or thereabouts is by Same Court bound unto Peter Hyatt Untill he the said John shall arrive to Age and the said Peter in his proper person in Court here promises to Learn the said Orphan during the Time afd to Read Dinstinctly in the Bible and at the Expiration thereof to give him a decent Suit of Apparel and an hoe of Each Sort and an Axe.

March 1746
DD 406
BROOKE, Benjamin:-is by the Court here admitted to Choose his Guardian and thereupon he makes Choice of John Bowie of Prince Georges County Planter who in his proper person in Court here declares his willingness to Accept the same.

August 1726
N 8
BROOKE, Walter:-(son of Thomas Brooke of Prince Georges County Gent) aged as tis said about nineteen years comes into Court here in his proper person and on his prayer is allow[d] by

the Court here to choose his Guardian whereupon he makes choice of his father abovenam'd,
and the said Thomas in his proper person also
in Court here declaring his willingness to
undertake the Guardianship of his said son
is by the Court here admitted thereunto-

August 1723   BROWN, Alice:-two years old the 24 day of
L 132   last January is by the Court here bound to
               Thomas Timson and Catherine his wife untill
               she arrive to the age of 16 years and there-
               upon the said Thomas as well for himself as
               his said wife in Court here engages to learn
               the said Alice to read distinctly in the Bible
               and at the Expiration of her time to give her
               a decent suit of apparell-

November 1716 BROWN, Benjamin:-Mary Brown by Consent of
H 141   this Court binds her Son Benjamin Brown to
               John Wall and Elizabeth his wife their heirs
               and Assignes till he Come to Age being Eight
               months old this day-

November 1739 BROWN, Henry:-born ye twenty-fourth Day of
X 501   March last past is by ye Court here Bound
               to John Crampton until he ye sd Henry arrive
               to ye Age of twenty one Years & ye sd John
               in Court here promises to use his Endeavor
               during ye term afd to learn ye sd Henry to
               read & at ye Expiration thereof to give him
               a decent Suit of Apparel-

November 1725 BROWN, John:-aged 14 years and an half (as
L 511   tis said) comes into Court here in his proper
               person and on his prayer is allowed by the
               Court to choose his guardian. Whereupon he
               makes choice of his God Father Robert Couts'

of the County afd and he the said Robert in
his proper person in Court here declaring his
willingness to undertake the guardianship of
the said John is by the Justices of the Court
here admitted thereunto.

March 1735
V 294

BROWN, Mary:-The petition of John George, humb-
ly Sheweth That Your Petitioner haveing out
of Christian Charity for three Years Past
Maintained a Poor Orphan Girl named Mary Brown
who was left Destitute of any friend or Re-
lation but Thomas Hill who is her uncle...&
she haveing not Any Estate Save Ninty Acres
of Land which is now in possession of Said
uncle, Which was not by the Will of Either
the Father or Mother of said Girl for they
both Dyed Intestate only that he Lived on the
Land wth the Mother at the Time of her Decease
& so has Continued Ever Since but now is Willing to quit his pretentiance Provided this
Worshipfull Court Will Please to let the
child Continue wth the Petitioner till she
Comes of age... ...Mary Brown put Under Care
of Petitioner, et al.

November 1726
N 105

BROWN, Samuel:-born the tenth day of July
Anno Dni seventeen hundred and twelve is by
the Court here bound to Samuel Sweringen untill he come to the age of twenty-one years,
whereupon the same Samuel Sweringen in his
proper person in Court here promises to give
him the said Lad at the Expiration of his
time a decent Suit of apparel and an heifer.

June 1697
A 164

BROWNE, Christopher:-sonn to Jane Browne being
ye base borne child with the consent of his
Mother is bound unto Christopher Thompson

untill he arrives to 21 yeares of age-to learne
to Reade-at expiration two Suits of Cloaths
the one to be Korsy ye other to be Serge...Jane
Browne, Servant woman to Christopher Thompson...
it did appeare to the Court that the Child was
not gott in this Country.

November 1720
K 11

BROWNE, Proctor:-is by the Court here bound
unto Samuel Breshears Senr and his Heirs untill he comes to the age of twenty one years,
And the said Samuel in Considn of the childs
being kept and maintained by him one year allready is allowed two hundred pounds of Tob^{o}
this present Levy. Whereupon he engages himselfe to learn the Said Proctor to read.

November 1721
K 419

BRYAN, Elizabeth:-Ordered that Terence Bryan
on his Petition be allowed five hundred pounds
of Tobacco this Levy towards maintaining his
Daughter Elizabeth.

April 1738
X 109

BRYAN, Philip:-aged (as tis said in Court here
Sixteen Years the first day of february Next
is by the Court here Bound to Oliver Harris
until he the sd Philip Arrives to the Age of
Twenty one Years in Consideration whereof the
sd Oliver in his proper person in open Court
promises during the Term afd to Learn the sd
Philip to Read & Write & at the Expiration
thereof to give him a decent Suit of apparell.

August 1721
K 372

BRYAN, Tho:-Terence Bryan in his proper person
in Court here binds his son named Tho Bryan
aged five years the first day of September
next to George Clagett untill the said Lad
come to the age of Twenty one years whereupon
the said George in Court here Engages to give
the said Thomas a years schooling and a decent

suit of apparell at ye Expiration of his time.

November 1703
B 262a
BUCK, Edward:-Servt to Mr. Clem^t Hill adjudged to be Eighteen years of age ordered thereupon ye said Fellon Serve ye said Clement Hill according to an Act of Assembly in Such cases made & provided.

March 1745
DD 20
BUCKLEY, Michael:-Aged (as it is said) Tenn Years is by the Court here bound to James Plummer of Prince Georges County Planter for and During the Term of Eleven years and the said James Plummer in his Proper person in Court here Promises to give the said Michael Buckley during the Term afd one years Schooling and at the Expiration of his time of Servitude freedom dues According to Act of Assembly.

November 1748
KK 36
BURGESS, Ann:-James Haddock Waring is by the Court here Appointed Gardian to Ann Burgess and the said James Haddock Waring present in Court here in his proper person Declares his Willingness to Accept that trust.

November 1748
KK 34
BURGES, Basil:-Francis Waring Gentleman (on his motion) is by the Court here appointed Gardian to Basil Burges.

June 1707
C 149
BURGESS, John:-als Thomas Box a Malatta Basterd of Margery Burges Servant to John Smith Eleven years Old October next is bound by the Court to Mr. Thomas Gant to Serve according to Law Mr. Robert Owen by his Letter to ye Court and Entered in Folio 147 of this booke relinguisheth any Right or Title he hath as minister of St. Pauls Parrish to the said Malatta boy...
Folio 147:=Whereas Severall Years Since a Servant woman belonging to Mr. John Smith had a Mallatta basterd Child wch By ye then Law was

appropriated to ye Minister of ye Parrish
and for as much as that crime was Committed
before my Arrivall and Mrs. Ann Wight hath
been att great Trouble in Raysing up the
Said Childe I doe hereby revoke & give up
any right title or Claime I have or ought
to have of in or to the said malatta Childe.
Wittness my hand ye Day abovesaid.R^t Owen

November 1748
KK 35

BURGESS, Ursula:-Thomas Waring is by the
Court here appointed Gardian to Ursula Burgess and the said Thomas Waring present
here in Court in his proper person Declares
his willingness to accept of that trust.

August 1728
O 334b

BURROUGHS, James:-nine months old is by the
Court here bound to William Ducker until he
the said James arrive to age and the said
William present here in Court in his proper
person promises to Learn the said James
during the term afd to read and to bring
him up to the art and mystery of a Tailor
and at the Expiration of his time to give
him a decent suit of apparell and in consideration of the childs Infancy the said
William is allowed in present Levy twelve
hundred pounds of Tobacco.

November 1734
V 213

BURROUGHS, James:-Mary Burroughs in Court here
binds her Son James Burroughs Twelve years
old the ninth Day of December next unto Daniel Freeman until the said James arrive to
Age. Whereupon the said Daniel in Open Court
Obliges himself to Learn the said James During the Term to Read and Write as also the
Art and Mystery of a Weaver and at the Expiration of the time to give him a Weaving Loom

and Gear and a Decent Suit of Apparel.

August 1731
R 220

Burton, Mary:-four years old the twenty fifth
of last March is by the Justices of the Court
here bound to John Jones until she arrive to
age & the said John Jones's wife (the husband
being at this time sick) ingages in Court
here during the term afsd to learn the said
Mary to read & at the expiration thereof to
give her a decent Suit of Apparel.

June 1697
A 189

BUSEY, Henry:- "I Ann Ewens am willing to
bind over my Sonn Henry Busey unto Hugh
Furguson, Surgion in Prince Georges County-
being Eleven yeares of age the 15 day of
July next the date hereof whilst he is 21
years of Age.   13 May 1697
wit George (x) Bussey, John (x) Harrington
"The Opinion of ye Court is it doth not
Lye in power of the Justices of this Court
to bind ye sd child by Reason his parents
Lives in Calvt County & his Father in Law
is not willing to the Same.

March 1750
LL 134

BUSSEY, Hezekiah:-Aged about Eleven Years
is by the Court here bound to Alexander
Magruder near Mill Town till he Arrive to the
Age of Twenty one years and the said Alexander Magruder agrees to give the Said Hezekiah a years Schooling And the Customary
freedom Dues at the Expiration of his Time
of Servitude.

June 1726
L 636

BUTLER, Thomas:-(son of James Butler deceased) aged as tis said 18 years or thereabouts came into Court here in his proper
person and on his prayer is allowed by the
Court here to Choose his guardian--whereupon

he makes choice of James Carroll of Annarundle
County Gent and the said James Carroll in
his proper person in Court here declaring his
willingness to undertake the Guardianship
of the said Thomas is by the Court here admitted thereunto.

November 1729   BYRNE, Edward:-a poor boy aged as tis said
four years next March is by the Justices of
the Court here bound to John Bradford until
age who in Consideration thereof in his proper
person in Court here promises to Learn the
boy to read and write during the term aforesaid and at the Expiration thereof to give
him a decent Suit of Apparell.

March 1707 CADDICK, Elizabeth:- 2½ years
C 127 CADDICK, Margaret:- 4½ years, Daughters to
Sarah Caddick bound to Mr. William Joseph
till age-

November 1747 CAIN, Jeremiah:-aged (as 'tis said) about
GG 281 two years in August last by the Court here
bound to Charles Higginbotham & Margaret
his wife untill age of Twenty one years
and the said Charles Higginbotham in Court
here on his part Covenants to learn or Cause
the said Orphan to be Learn'd to read & at
the Expiration of time to give them the Customary Freedom dues-

November 1735 CALVIN, John:- aged as it is said in Court
V 620 here Sixteen Years the 9th Instant is by the
Court here admitted to Choose his Guardian
whereupon he makes Choice of Henry Tren(n)
of Prince Georges Co., planter who in his
proper person in Court here Declares his
Willingness to Accept the same-

June 1716 CAMBELL, Joseph:- Son of Catherine Cambell
H 85 by Consent of the Coart is bound to Elizabeth Gerrard till he Attain the Age of
twenty-one years the said Elizabeth Gerrard
to learn him to read and give him a Suite
of Cloaths-

March 1738 CAMDEN, Richard:-a Motherless Boy (son of
W 652 John Camden Sometime Since Runaway) aged
14 yrs the 31 Day of March Instant is by
the Court here bound to John Jakey until he
the sd Richard arrive to ye age of 21 years
---agreement---a years schooling & to use
his utmost indeavour to learn him the Trade
& mystery of a Cordwainer & at the Expir-

he makes choice of James Carroll of Annarundle
County Gent and the said James Carroll in
his proper person in Court here declaring his
willingness to undertake the Guardianship
of the said Thomas is by the Court here admitted thereunto.

November 1729   BYRNE, Edward:-a poor boy aged as tis said
four years next March is by the Justices of
the Court here bound to John Bradford until
age who in Consideration thereof in his proper
person in Court here promises to Learn the
boy to read and write during the term aforesaid and at the Expiration thereof to give
him a decent Suit of Apparell.

November 1733
S 473

CHEW, Joseph, Jr.:- (a minor as tis said) prays the Justices of the Court here that he may be admitted to Choose his guardian which is granted him, whereupon he makes choice of Joseph Chew, Gent., his father, who upon his Declaring in Court here his Willingness to accept the same is admitted accordingly-

June 1727
N 354

CLARK, John:- (Son of Alexander & Rachel Clark both Deceased) three years old next September is by the Court here bound to Benjamin Osborn...until he the said Orphan arrive to the age of twenty one years & in Consideration thereof the said Benjamin in his proper person in Court here obliges himself to Learn the said Orphan during the time afd to read distinctly & at the Expiration thereof to give him a Decent Suit of apparell-

June 1727
N 347

CLARK, Mary:- (Daughter of Alexander & Rachel Clark both deceased) born the nineteenth day of March Anno Dm Seventeen hundred & twenty-five is by the Court here bound to Thomas Tumpson & Catherine his wife Until it come to the age of Sixteen years & in Consideration of its infancy the said Thomas is allowed in the next County Levy twelve hundred pounds of Tobacco whereupon the said Thomas in his proper person in Court here promises during the term afd to Learn the said Mary to read distinctly & at the Expiration thereof to give her a decent Suit of Apparell-

August 1748
HH 337

CLARVO, Henry:- comes into Court and makes Choice of Edward Pearson for his Guardian who by Letter to the Same Court has signified

his Willingness to Accept of that Trust
which letter the Justices of the Court here
order to be Recorded Vizt., To the Worships
of Prince Georges Cty now Sitting These are
to Certifie I am not able to Come up to
Court my Self but in case Henry Clarvo(Neavu)
to my Wife choses me as Guardian I am Content
to doe my Duty as far as I am able both for
his body and Estate if your Worship pleases
to order it I have Sent up Security on pur-
pose for the Same I am your humble Servt to
Commd- Aug ye 24 1748 Edwd X Pearson

March 1746
FF 385

CLAYTON, Thomas:- aged (as tis said) Seven
years is by the Court here bound to Humphry
Whitmore untill he arrive to the Age of
Twenty one years. And the said Humphry Whit-
more in Court here promises to give the said
Thomas Clayton one years Schooling and at
the Expiration of his time a decent suit of
Apparell-

September 1699
A 474

CLIFFOARD, John:- base borne Child of Abigaile
Clifford by ye Consent of his mother he being
then five months old was bound out to Edward
Willett or his assignes till he arive to ye
age of one and twenty years of age-

June 1701
B 111

CLIFFORD, Elizabeth:- aged 4 years old ye
4th day of November Last by ye consent of
her Mother Abigaile Clifford was bound to
Edward Willett till she arive to ye age of
Sixteen years old-

August 1713
G 385

COLEBRON, Joseph:- by consent of his Father
Francis Colebron is bound to Richard Duckett
and his Assignes till he Attaine ye Age of
One and Twenty Yeares he being five yrs old

25

ye Fourteenth of Mar last year & The sd
Richard Duckett to doe his Endeavour to
Learne him to read in ye Bible and at ye
Expiration of the sd Terme the said Rich^d
Duckett or his Assignes to give and deliver
unto the sd Joseph Colebron One Suite of
Cloathes That is to Say Coate & Briches
and Waist Coate Hats Shirt Shoes and
Stockings-

August 1698
A 332

COLLINGS, Morgan:- Servt to John Barrott
adjudged nineteen years ordered to serve
according to act of assembly-

June 1716
H 85

COOKE, Jeremiah:- Son of Thomas Cooke by
Consent of the Court is bound to Edward
and Mary Marlow till he attain the Age of
Twenty-one years and if the said Edward
and Mary Marlow Shall happen to dye before
the Expiration of the aforesaid term of
twenty-one years then the said Jeremiah
Cooke to serve the remaining part of his
time with Ralph Marlow he the said Jeremiah Cooke being Ten years of age this Day
and to have two years Schooling given him
by the said Marlow and at the Expiration of
his time of Servitude to have a new Suite
of Serge or Sagathie two White Shirts a
pair of new Shooes and Stockins one new hatt-

August 1748
HH 341

COX, John:- comes into Court and makes Choice
of Abraham Cox for his Guardian who in Court
here declares his Willingness to Accept of
that Trust-

November 1722
K 650

CRAWFORD, Susannah:- an orphan Eleven years
old ye fifteenth of July last is by ye Court

here bound unto Edward Dawson Junr untill
She arrive to age whereupon ye sd Edward
in Court here Oblidges himselfe to give ye
sd Susannah a decent suit of apparel according to act of Assembly at the Expiration of
her time-

March 1709 D 149	CREYCROFT, John:-Sonn of ye Late Mr. Ignatius Craycroft came into Court and made Choyce of Mr. Luke Gardiner to be his Guardian-
June 1710 D 316	CROAMY, James: Sevt to Mr. Robert Owen ad- judged to be 12 years of age, Ordered that ye said James Serve ye Said Mr. Owen accord- ing to act of Assembly in that Case Made & Provided-
September 1701 B 137	CROSS, Ann Joyce:- an Orphn Child borne the Last of Aprill 1701 was bound by her Sup- posed Father James Cross till 16 years of age or day of mariage to John Chapman-
November 1744 CC 585	CROSS, Robert:- (son of Margaret Cross) aged (as tis said) Tenn Months is by the Court here bound to John Rawlings of Prince Georges County Planter until he arrive to the Age of Twenty one years and the said John Rawlings in his Proper Person in Court here undertakes to give the said Robert Cross during the Term aforesaid one years Schooling and at the Ex- piration thereof the usual freedom Dues-
March 1715 G 720	CULLIN, Charles:- Elizabeth Cullin by Consent of ye Court binds her Son Charles Cullin to John Rea and Mary his wife, till he attaine ye Age of Twenty One years being three years old ye Sixteenth day of February last-
March 1718 H 798	CULLIN, Charles:- Son of Dennis Cullin and Elizabeth Cullin is by consent of the Court

bound to George Wilson and Agnes his wife, till he attains the age according to Law being now Six years old, to give him a years schooling, and a compleat suite of apparell of Broad cloth with all things fitting thereunto-

November 1726
N 108

CUMBERLAND, James:- son of John and Mary Cumberland born the twenty-eighth of February seventeen hundred and twenty-one is by the Court here bound to Francis Wheat his Godfather untill he the said James arrive to the age of Twenty one years and hereupon the said Francis present here in Court in his proper person promises and obliges himself to give his said Godson during the term afd two years Schooling and at the Expiration thereof a decent suit of Apparell-

June 1726
L 652,653

CUMBERLAND, John:- is by the Justices of the Court here bound to his afsd Godfather Thomas Stonestreet untill he the said John shall arrive to the age of 21 years and the said Thomas in Court here promises to give the said Godson during the time afd one year and an half schooling and at the expiration of it a decent suit of Cloaths and a young mare and in case of the sd Thomas Stonestreets death the said John is then to remain the rest of his time with his other Godfather Richard Durham who in Court here promises to fullfill what shall be undone of the above recited conditions on the part of the said Thomas Stonestreet to be performed towards the said orphan in case he come to him the said Richard Durham-

March 1725
L 558

CUMBERLAND, William:- aged 16 years next
November or thereabouts is by the Justice
of the Court here bound to William Wallace
untill he the said William Cumberland arrive
to the age of 21 years---agreement---William
Wallace in his proper person in court obliges
himself to give the said Lad at the Expiration a decent suit of apparell and a Cow
and Calf a young horse and young mare in
lieu of those Creatures he has now in his
Custody belonging to the said William Cumberland as also during the afd time to learn
him to read and write-

March 1744
CC 270

DALTON, John:- an Orphan Aged (as tis said) Nine years the first Day of January last is by the Court here bound to Butler Stonestreet & his Assigns until he Arrive to the Age of Twenty one years And the said Butler Stonestreet in his Proper Person in Court here Promises During the Term aforesaid to give the said John Dalton one years Schooling and at the Expiration of his Time a Decent Suit of Apparel-

March 1711/1712
G 291

DAVIS, George:- being Eight yeares Old the Nineth day of August next,

DAVIS, John:- being five Yeares old the fourth day of October next-

being both sons of Gregory Davis by Consent of their Mother Margaret Davis is bound to John Williams of Roock Creek and Sarah his Wife till they Severally attaine their Age & according to Acts of Assembly. And the said John Williams Doe for himselfe and Sarah his Wife promise and agree to give the said Children George and John Davis each of them a yeares Schooling and to each of them at the Expiration of their time of Servitude One Suite of Cloathes (that is to say) either of Kersey or Brood Cloath as allsoe Shirts Shooes and Stockings and One Hatt to each of them-

November 1734
V 225

DENIOSIA, Edward:- Mary Miles in Court here binds her grand son Edward Deniosia Aged Eleven years the Thirteenth Day of January next unto Jeremiah Perdue Until he the said Edward arrive to Age and the said Jeremiah

in Court here promises to Learn the Said
Edward During the Term af'd to Read Distinctly
in the Bible and at the Expiration thereof
to Give him a Decent Suit of apparel-

June 1704
B 300

DEVALL, Benjamin:- aged Eighteen years
came into Court and made Choyce of
Mr. Robert Tyler to be his Guardian-

November 1698
A 355

DHOLOHUNDAE, John:- Servt to Murphey Ward
adjudged to be 18 years old & to Serve according to Act of assembly-

March 1730
R 5

DICK, Male Child:- Priscilla Gray alias
Malatto Priscilla's Male Child named Dick
aged about three months is by the Justices
of the Court here bound unto Lingan Wilson
until it arrive to the age of Twenty one
years-

June 1702
B 163

DIMHUE, Mary, alius Godfrey:- aged 3 years
of age come August next was by ye request
of Godfery Barnes bound to Ann Smith till
age or ye Day of Marriage-

September 1701
B 137

DONNELL, David:- Servant to John Henry adjudged to be ffourteen years of age Ordered
that he Serve his said Master according to
Law-

August 1747
GG 96

DOWNING, Terence:- aged as tis said Fourteen months in October next is by the Court
here bound unto Philip Mason untill he arrives
to the age of Twenty one Years in consideration whereof the said Philip Mason promises
& oblidges himself to Learn or cause him the
said Terence Downing to be learned to read
distinctly and to write and at the Expiration
of his time of Servitude to furnish him with
freedom Dues agreeable to Law and Custom of

this Province-

November 1745
DD 265

DYATT, Elizabeth:- Anne Dyatt on her Death
bed before (illeg) Evidences gave her Daughter Elizabeth to your Petitioner Ninian Mar-
iarte-being Godfather to the said Girl wch
yr Worships bound last Court to Wm. Proctor
unknown to your Petitioner by reason of
Sickness yt he could not attend your Worships
so bed your Worships will bind ye sd Girl to
your Pet^r & in duty bound he will pray & c.-

August 1745
DD 185

DYE, Elizabeth:- aged (as it is said) nine
years last May is by the Court here bound
unto the Petitioner (William Proctor) until
she arrive to the age of Sixteen Years and
the said William Proctor in his Proper person
in Court here undertakes at the Expiration
of her time of Servitude to give her the
freedom dues according to the Custom of
Servants Imported into this Province-

November 1711
G 124

DYER, Penelope:- Comes into open Court and
is bound to Thomas Edelen till She Attaine
the Age of Sixteene years. She being Eight
years old the Twenty fourth day of February
next-

November 1711
G 124

DYER, William:- Sonn of Pattrick Dyer Comes
into Court and is bound to Thomas Edelen till
he attaine the Age of Seaventeene years being
Six years old the Eighteenth day of this instant: And then the said Thomas Edeln is
hereby obliged to bind the said William Dyer
to such Trade as he shall then make Choyse
of till he attaine the age of Twenty one
years or as they shall agree-

March 1701 B 94	EDELIN, Christopher:- aged 18 years appeared in Open Court & made Choyce of his Brother Thomas Edelin to be his Guardian till he arrive to ye age of one & 20 yrs. ye said Thomas to indevour to cause him to Read & wright-
March 1710 D 276	EDGAR, Elizabeth:- EDGAR, Sarah:- Richard Edgar desires to have his childrens Age recorded as vizt., Sarah & Elizabeth Edgar Twinns Daughters of Richd Edgar & Joanna his wife of Prince Georges were born ye Eight & Twenty Day of October in the yeare of our Lord one Thous- and Seven hundred & six-
August 1702 B 168	EDWARDS, John:- Servant to William Barton adjudged to be fourteen years of age- Ordered he Serve according to Law-
November 1726 N 106	EELE, male child:- A male child of Mary Eele's eleven weeks old the twenty seventh of this instant is by the Court here bound to John Breshears (son of Samuel Breshears) until it come to the age of twenty-one years and in consideration of its infancy the said John is allow^d four hundred pounds of To- bacco in the present Levy whereupon the afd Master promises in Court here to learn the said Child to read distinctly in the Bible in case as it grows up it do not prove a ma- latto (void) her Tryal-
March 1712 G 174	ELSON, Nicholas:- Sonn of William Elson by Consent of his Mother Anne Elson is bound to Andrew Webster and his wife till he at- taine the age of Twenty one years being

Eleven years old the Second day of Aprill
next. The said Webster to give him two
years Schooling And doe his utmost endeavour
to learne him the Trade of Taylor, and at
the Expiracon of his aforesd Time the said
Andrew Webster or Wife & c., to give and deliver unto the said Nicholas Elson one Suite
of Cloathes and Shirts Shooes & Stockins-

November 1714
G 691

EVANS, Elizabeth:- Comes into open Court
and Chuses Mr. Benjamine Hall Guardian:
...said Elizabeth Evans being above the Age
of fourteene years-

March 1735
V 292,293

EVANS, Harding:- fourteen years Old the
Fourteenth Day of this Instant March and
William Kitchin Nine Years Old this Ninth
Day of Last October Two Orphan Lads are by
the Court here bound unto Caleb Litton Until
they the Said Lads shall respectively Arrive
to Age and the Said Caleb in his proper person
in Court here obliges himself During the
Term afsd to Learn Each of the Said Ladds
to Read & Write-at Expiration...to Give Each
a Decent Suit of Apparel-

June 1743
AA 676

EVANS, John:- aged (as 'tis said) fourteen
Years the Sixth day of May last is by the
Court here bound to George Parker of Prince
Georges County Gent until he arrive to the
age of Twenty one Years and the said George
Parker in his proper Person in Court here
Promises during the term aforesaid to give
the said Evans one years Schooling and at
the Expiration of his time a Decent Suit of
Apparel-

November 1714
G 691

EVANS, Richard:- Mrs. Elizabeth Evans comes into open Court and prayes that Mr. Benjamin Hall may be appointed Guardian to Richard Evans her Sonn; he being under the age of ffourteene years; And accordingly the said Benjamin Hall is appointed by the Curt(sic) to be Guardian to the said Richard Evans-

November 1714
G 691

EVANS, Samuell:- Comes into open Court and Chuses Mr. Benjamine Hall Guardian:... said Samuell Evans being above the Age of fourteene years-

November 1724
L 376,377

FALBY, Esther:- Honoria Falby in her proper person in Court here binds her daughter Esther Falby being three years old the 29th day of next Aprill unto Caleb Litton untill the said Esther arrive to the age of 16 years and the said Caleb in his proper person here engages himself to learn the said Esther to read and at the Expiration of her time to give her a Decent Suit of Apparell-

November 1729
P 250

FALCONER, John:- (an Orphan) aged as 'tis said fourteen years the twenty fifth day of next February is by the Justices of the Court here bound to John Edgar until age who in Consideration thereof in his proper person in Court here promises to learn the said Orphan boy to read and write during the term afsd and at the Expiration thereof to give him a decent Suit of apparell-

November 1729
P 250

FALCONER, William:- (an Orphan) aged as tis said Six years next April is by the Justices of the Court here bound to Richard Wade until age who in Consideration thereof in his proper person in Court here promises to Learn the said Orphan boy to read and write during the term afsd and at the Expiration thereof to give him a decent suit of apparell-

November 1711
G 124

FFARMER, John:- Sonn of William ffarmer was in open Court bound to Samuell ffarmer till he attaine the Age of Twenty-one yeares he being Thirteene years old next August the said Samuell ffarmer being Obliged to learne or cause the said John ffarmer to read in the Bibble-

November 1709
D 249
FARMER, Mary:- an orphant childe of William Farmer Deceased Aged Eight years old the fifth day of March Last Past bound to James Gladstone till Age or day of Marriage-

June 1716
H 84
FARMER, Samuell:- Son of William Farmer by Consent of the Court is bound to Robert Wheeler till he attain the Age of Twenty-one years according to Act of Assembly... he being twelve years of Age the first day of December next-

August 1730
P 453
FITCHELL, Elizabeth:- the Daughter of Margaret Fitchell is by the Court here bound to John Rogers until she come to age & in consideration of the Childs Infancy it is ordered by the Court here that the said John Rogers be allowed Eight hundred pounds of Tobacco in the next County Levy whereupon he promises to give the said Elizabeth during the term afsd a years Schooling if he has the Conveniency & at the Expiration thereof a Decent Suit of apparell-

November 1720
K 8
FLANN, Francis:- about eighteen months olde by Consent of the Court here bound to John Piles or his assigns untill he arrive to the age of twenty-one years, In consideration whereof the said John Piles oblidges himselfe to learn the said Child to read distinctly, and at the expiration of the Term to give him a good decent Suite of apparell-

November 1745
DD 277
FLATFOOT, Sarah:- the Daughter of John Flatfoot aged (as tis said) twelve Years is by the Court here bound to Elizabeth Kirkwood until she arrive to the Age of Sixteen years

& the said Elizabeth Kirkwood in her Proper
Person in Court here undertakes during the
Term aforesaid to learn the aforesaid Sarah
to read & at the Expiration of her time to
give her the freedom dues allowed from Masters
to Servants Imported into this Province-

June 1718
H 670

FLEMAN, William:- Ordered that William Fleman
Son of Ann Fleman by consent of his Mother
is bound to William Mordent and Anne his Wife
till he come to age according to Act of Assembly. He being four years old the Third
Day of Octo^r next, The said William Mordent
and Anne his wife to doe their best indeav-
ours to learn or cause to be learned the said
William Fleman to write and read as also to
give him one Suite of cloths Two Shirts and
a pair of shoes and stockings One hatt at
the expiration of the aforesaid time-

June 1732
R 522

FLETCHER, Sarah:- five years old (as it is
said) the first day of May last is by the
Court here at the assent of her Mother Hannah Jefferies bound unto Richard Pickleton
of Prince Georges County Merchant until she
the said Sarah arrive to the age of Sixteen
years & the said Richard Pickleton in his
proper person in open Court promises to
Learn the said Sarah during the term af'd
to read & at the expiration thereof to give
her a decent Suit of Apparel-

November 1715
H 6

FLOOD, Jane:-being ten years Old last August
FLOOD, Margarett:-two years and halfe old
this Court---by Consent of the Court bound
to Archibald Edmondson and his Heirs till

they Severally attaine their Ages according
to Act of Assembly-

June 1700
B 53

FFOREST, John:- Elizabeth Perry Binds her
Sonn John Fforest Aged 4 years Last Febry
to Tho Gibbons untill he arrive to ye age
of One & 20 years-

June 1698
A 317

FORREST, Ellinor:- Elizabeth Forrest widow
came into Court and bound her Daughter
named Ellinor Forrest unto Mr. William Barton
untill 16 Ellinor being 12 yeare old 2 January next-

June 1698
A 317

FORREST, Lucy:- Elizabeth Forrest widow
came into Court and bound her daughter Lucy
unto Mr. William Barton untill 16 Lucy
being 8 yeares of age 23 December next-

June 1739
X 344

FOSSET, Thomas:- (as tis sd) four Years Old
ye latter end of March last Son of John Fosset is by ye Court here bound unto Charles
Bowman untill ye sd Thomas Fosset Arrive to
ye Age of Twenty-one years & the sd Charles
Bowman in Court here promises to learn ye
sd. Thos. Fosset during ye Term afd to read
Distinctly in ye Bible & at ye Expiration
thereof to give him a decent Suit of apparel-

November 1727
N 612

FOSSETT, John:- a Dumb Ladd three years old
this day to wit the twenty ninth day of November in the twelfth year of his Lordships
the Lord Proprietarys Dominion & of the consent of his Mother Jane Fossett present here
in Court is by the Court here bound to Thomas
Johnson until he the said John arrive to the
age of twenty-one years, hereupon the said
Thomas present here in Court in his proper

person obliges himself to give the said
minor at the Expiration of the said Term a
Decent Suit of Apparel-

November 1725   FOWLER, John:- a poor helpless orphan 7 weeks
L 511,512   old the 29 day of this instant November is
by the Justices of the Court here bound unto
Charles Anderson until It Comes to the age
of 21 years and the said Charles in consideration of the childs infancy is allow^{d} 1200
pds of Tobacco in the Present Levy-

January 1706   GAMBLIN, Elizabeth:- Eleven years of Age
C 110a   Chose Gabb[11] Burnam Junior her Brother
                in Law to be her Guardian

August 1703   GAMBLIN, Mary:-
B 250   GAMBLING, Elizabeth:- John Anderson &
                Gabriell Burnam Senior of Prince Georges
                Co. doe acknowledge ourselves to stand Justly
                Indebted unto Mary Gamblin & unto Elizabeth
                Gambling, orphant Children unto James Gambling
                Lately deceased in ye full and just Sume of
                195 pounds & 1 shilling- 10 July 1703-

March 1724   GIBBS, Andrew:- (son of James & Mary Gibbs)
L 413,414   born Feb 12 1717 is by Court bound to Thomas
                Stonestreet his God father untill he the said
                Andrew comes to age of 21 years-said Thomas
                engages to Learn his said God-Son to read
                distinctly in the Bible and at the Expira-
                tion of his time to give him a Decent Suit
                of Apparell-

March 1724   GIBBS, James:- (Son of James & Mary Gibbs
L 413   Deceased) born February 23, 1709 chooses
                William Webster as Guardian-

March 1724   GIBBS, Jane:- (another Daughter of James &
L 413   Mary Gibbs dec) born Aug 31, 1720 by the
                Justices of the Court bound to William Web-
                ster to 16 years- William in Court here en-
                gages to Learn the said Girl to read and at
                the Expiration of her time to give her a
                Decent suit of Apparell

November 1728   GIBBS, Jannett:- a poor helpless orphan is
O 331   by the court here bound to John Bennett until
                she arrive to age and the said John in con-
                sideration of the said Jennett her Infancy is

allowed in the present Levy Sixteen hundred
pounds of Tobacco and hereupon he promises
to give the said Jennett at the Expiration
of her time a decent suit of apparell-

March 1724
L 413
GIBBS, Mary:- born January 3, 1714, and
GIBBS, Mary Ann:- born July 13, 1712
(Daughters of James and Mary Gibbs, Dec.)
bound to William Webster by the Justices of
the Court to 16 years- William in Court here
engages to Learn the said Girls to read and
at the Expiration of their time to give them
a Decent suit of Apparell-

March 1724
L 413
GIBBS, Philip:- (son of James & Mary Gibbs)
born 9 Feb 1707 chooses Henry Barns for his
Guardian-

August 1727
N 496
GIBBS, Philip:- Aged as tis said twenty years
the ninth day of next February in his proper
person in Court here makes Choice of William
Webster for his Guardian as afd & the said
William in Court here likewise declaring his
willingness to undertake the Guardianship
of the said Philip is by the Court here admitted thereunto-

August 1711
G 78
GILBORN, Elizabeth:- Daughter of William and
Dorothy Gilborn by Consent of the Court is
bound to Edward Phenix and Wife till she at-
taine the age of Sixteene yeares She now being
Six years and ffour months old and the said
Edward Phenix and Wife to doe theire Endeavour
to learne her to read in the Bible-

August 1710
G 25
GILBURNE, Sarah:- Daughter to Wm. and Mary
Gilburne tenn years of age ye tenth day of
June last past bound to Mr. Deheniossa till
age or day of marriage but if ye Said Dehen-

42

iosa Depart out of ye Province ye said Sarah
to be ffree ye said Sarah to be taught to
read and doe plaine Sewing worke-

March 1717
H 182

GODDARD, John:- is by consent of the Court
bound to Thomas Stonestreet till he come to
Age he being Thirteen Years old last October
the said Stone Street to give him a Years
Schooling and to learn him the Carpenters
trade and to give him at the Expiration of
his time of Servitude a new Suit of Apparell-

June 1710
D 318

GORDON, Peter:- Servant to Mr. James Wallace
adjudged to be 13 years old: Ordered thereupon that ye said Gordin Serve ye said Wallace according to an Act of Assembly of this
province in that case made & provided-

November 1731
R 278

GOSLING, Robert:- aged as tis said fifteen
years the fourth day of November Instant is
by the Court here bound unto Owen Ellis until
he the said Robert Gosling arrive to the age
of Twenty one years & the said Owen Ellis in
his proper person in Court here promises to
use his utmost indeavour by himself personally
during the time afd to learn the said Robert
Gosling to write & at the expiration of the
term to give him a suit of Cloth drugget two
dowlas Shirts, a pair of Shoes & Stockins a
Castor hat a neck cloth & pair of gloves, two
hoes & an axe & an heifer bigg with Calf-

March 1750
LL 135

GOWIN, Charles:- Aged about four years is
Bound to Henry Watson Jun till he arrive to
the Age of Twenty one years And the said Henry
Watson Agrees to give the said Charles Gowin
a years Schooling and the Customary freedom

Dues at the Expiration Of his Time of Servitude and Joseph Belt Jun Gent. in his Proper
person in Court undertakes to See the Conditions afsd performed-

August 1724
L 334

GRAHAM, Mary:- Elizabeth Graham in her
proper person in Court here binds her daughter
Mary Graham three years old the Tenth day of
next November to James Young until the girl
come to the age of 16 years whereupon the
said James in Court here likewise ingages
himself to learn the Child to read distinctly
in the Bible and at expiration to give her
a Decent Suit of apparel-

June 1703
B 249

GREEN, Elizabeth:- orphant of John Green &
his wife deceased taken from William Prather,
She being 13 mos old now at this time and
bound to John Henry till she arives to ye age
of Sixteen or the day of marriage and in Consideration thereof to have twelve hundred
pounds of Tobacco ye next Leavy and the year
following to have 800 pds of Tobacco and for
ye ffewture to have noe ffurther allowance-

June 1707
C 149

GREEN, Hugh:- an Orphant Childe of John Green
deceased Six years old ye next October bound
to Mr. Robt Tyler till age the said Tyler
obleidges himself to give him Sufficient
Schooleing That is to Say to Read and write
and at ye Expiration of his time to give him
the freedom Rights of this Province and a Cow
and Calfe and in Case ye Said Tyler Deceaseth
before ye Expiration of ye said Greens Indented
Time that he Continue Edward Tyler Sonn of
the sd Robert Tyler-

November 1696 A 61	GREENE, Thomas:- Sonn of Leonard Greene came into Court & desired that Francis Marbary may bee Recorded his Guardian to take Care of him & what is due to him-
June 1698 A 317	GREENDELL, Wm:- Servt to Murphy Ward adjudged 18 yrs of age-
June 1750 LL 176	GRIFFEN, Richard:- aged 11 years the 22 day of December next, and GRIFFEN, Thomas:- aged 14 years the 14 day of next January--Ordered by the Court bound unto Hezekiah Magruder Untill they arrive to the age of 21 years- Agreement, a years Schooling Each and the customary Freedom dues of the County at the Expiration of their Time of Servitude-
March 1745 DD 278	GRIMES, Ann:- the Daughter of Catherine Grimes (as tis said) Six Weeks is by the Court here bound to William Bowie until she arrive to the age of Sixteen years & in Consideration of its Infancy the said William Bowie is allowed five hundred pounds of Tobacco in the next County Levy-
March 1744 CC 275	GRIMES, John:- Aged (as it is said) Seven Years the Twenty fifthe Instant is by the Court here bound to William Willett of Prince Georges County Planter and his Assignes untill he arrive to the age of Twenty one years and the said William Willett in his Proper person in Court here Promises During the Term aforesaid to Learn the said John Grimes to read Distinctly in the Bible and at the Expiration of his time of Servitude to give him a Decent Suit of Apparel-
November 1743 CC 156	GRIMES, Philip:- an Orphan Aged (as tis said) three years is by the Court here bound to

William Willett and his Assignes untill he
Arrive to the Age of Twenty one years and
the said William Willett in his proper person in Court here Promises (During the term
aforesaid) to give the said Philip one years
Schooling and at the Expiration thereof to
give him a Decent Suit of Apparell-

June 1713

G 348

GUY, Jeremiah:- by Consent of ye Court is
bound unto Richard Isaac till he Attaine ye
Age of Twenty-one years he being nine years
old in this Instant June and at ye Expiration
of ye said Terme ye sd Isaac to give to ye
sd Guy One Two year old Heffer One young Sow
and One Suite of Cloaths and to learne him
to read-

June 1717
H 240

HALL, Margaret:- and Elizabeth Rogers is by
Consent of the Court bound to John Brent and
Elizabeth his wife and their Heirs till they
Severally attain their Ages According to Act
of Assembly The Said Margaret Hall being
fourteen years Old the Twenty Third Day of
January next the other five weeks old this
Day. The said John Brent to be Allowed for
keeping the young Child Twelve hundred pounds
of Tobacco next Levy Court and Eight Hundred
the year after-

June 1742
AA 3

HARBERT, William:- aged Eighteen years the
Eighteenth day of March next is by the Court
here admitted to Choose his Guardian and
hereupon he makes Choice of Alexander Harbert
Gent, who in Court in his Proper Person Declares his Willingness to accept the same-

June 1710
D 318

HARDIN, Thomas:- being now a yeare old bound
to Dan^{ll} Delozer till age-

November 1739
X 496

HARVEY, Thomas:- Aged (as it is sd) Sixteen
Years is by ye Court here Admitted to choose
his Guardian--hereupon he makes Choice of his
Uncle James Harvey of Prince Georges County
Planter who in Court here declares his Will-
ingness to Accept ye same-

June 1715
G 764

HAWKINS, James:- Ordered that James Hawkins
live with John Hawkins till he attaine the
Age of Twenty-One Years being fourteen years
old the Seventh day of March last past-

June 1735
V 401

HAY, Robert:- Aged as it is Said in Court here
nine years the 15 Day of November Last is by
the same Court Bound unto Edward Holmes of
Prince Georges County Planter until the Said
Robert Shall Arrive to Age the Said Edward in

his proper person in Court here-promises
during the Term afsd to Learn the Said Lad
to Read & Write - At Expiration to Give him
a Decent Suit of Apparell-

June 1715
G 764

HENLEY, Denis:- by Order of Court is bound
to James Brammell and his heirs till he attaine ye Age of Twenty One Years being now
nineteen months old And the said James Brammell to learn the said Dennis Henley the Art
of a Lawyer And when the said Dennis Henley's
time of Servitude is Expired as abovesaid
then the said James Brammell or his Heires
to give and deliver unto the said Dennis
a new Suite of Cloaths of Serge or Keersey
two white Shirts a New Hatt a pr of French
fall Shoes & one pair of Stockins and two
year old mare-

March 1716
H 33

HENLEY, Elizabeth:- Daughter of Daniel Henley by Consent of her Mother Mary Cole is
bound to Clement Hill & his now wife untill
she arrive to age according to Act of Assembly. She being Seaven years of age on
Twelfe Day last the said Clement Hill being
Appointed Elizabeth Henleys Gardian-

November 1720
K 11

HENLY, Mary:- is by the Court here bound
unto Thomas (Uray) untill she come to age,
Whereupon he oblidges himselfe to learn
her to read-

November 1747
GG 268

HENRIETTA:- Mary Peacock the wife of John
brings into Court here an Infant Girl whose
parents are unknown called Henrietta aged
about ten Months and the Court on mature Consideration do allow the aforesaid John Pea-

cock Two thousand pounds of Tobacco in the
next County Levy for his Trouble and care of
said Child to this time. And the Justices
of the same Court also bind the said Infant
to the same John Peacock untill she arrives
to the Age of Sixteen Years~

March 1728
O 16

HENRY, John:- Aged as tis said Thirteen
years next November bound unto William Shepherd until he the said John arrive to the
age of Twenty years Whereupon the said William in his proper person in Court here
promises to bring up the above named Lad to
the Carpenter trade and to give him a decent
Suit of apparel at the Expiration of his time-

March 1728
O 331

HENRY, Moses:- Aged as tis said Six years
the Twenty-seventh of March Instant is by the
Consent (of his father James Henry present
here in Court) bound unto William Shepherd
untill he the said Moses arrive to the Age
of twenty Years Whereupon the said William
in his proper person in Court here promises
to bring up the above named Lad to the Carpenters trade and to give him a decent Suit
of aparel at the Expiration of his time-

August 1715
G 786

HENWOOD, John:- by Consent of his Mother
Mary Henwood is bound unto William Nicholls
and his now wife till he attain the Age of
Eighteen Years being three years old the
Twenty Nineth day of May last past and the
said Wm. Nicholls & Wife to give him the
said John Henwood two Years Schooling & c.~

March 1723
L 4

HEYSTEHEART, Anna Catherina: 6 years of age
this day 28 March 1723, and

HEYSTEHEART, John Jacob:- 12, years of age
25 November last, and
HEYSTEHEART, John Lodewick:- 8 years of age
14 February last
Doct^r Richard Piles produces to the Court
here Sevts to be adjudged of their Ages namely
John Jacob Heysteheart, John Lodewick Heysteheart and Anna Catherina Heysteheart-

March 1711
G 43

HILL, Elizabeth:-, and
HILL, Mary:-

     Eliz. Hill an orphant of William and
Sarah Hill Deceased Twelve years of age ye
Sixth day of January next bound to Owen Ellis
and Mary Hill Daughter to ye said William &
Sarah four years of Age much about this time
bound to ye Said Ellis ye Said Ellis obleidgeing himselfe to Cause them to be Taught to Spin
and Card wooling and to Spin Linne and to Sow-

June 1697
A 162

HILL, Richard:- Elizabeth Hill Came into open
Court and binds her Sonn Richard Hill aged
Eight yeare ould in September next unto
Mr. Daniel Small to Serve him untill he Arrives unto twenty-one...to learne the said
boy to Read & write if possible he cann & to
give him at the Expiration of the said time
two Suits of Cloaths the one Kersey the other
Serge with two of a Sort of other necessary
apparrell-

September 1698
A 343

HINE, Mary:- 6 yrs of age in October next by
Consent of her Mother Hannah Hine bound to
serve Bartholomew Goff till 16 years of age...
to be learnt to read and to sow plaine worke
at Expiration of her time 2 suits of apparell
& other necessarys belonging to womans wareing

aparrell one Suit to be of Serge and the
other of Ponnistone-

August 1734   HOBBS, Anne:- Tenn years old the 28 day of
V 95   Last February, and
               HOBBS, Orson:-,
               HOBBS, Valentine:- Eight years old Tenth day
               of next September (being twins) are by the
               Court there of the Consent of their mother
               Joyce Hobbs present here in Court---bound
               unto Edward Swann of Prince Georges County,
               planter until they do respectively arrive to
               their Several Lawful Ages Provided their
               ffather in law James Shields his Consent is
               Obtained & produced in Court here During the
               Sessions- and the said Edward Swann produces
               to the Court here the following Certificate
               "This is to Satisfie your Worships that I de-
               sire the Children may be Bound to Edward Swan
               this from under my hand ye 28 Aug 1734"

                                    James (x) Shelds

August 1711   HODGES, Charity:- dau of Thomas Hodges by
G 78   consent of her Mother Charity Hodges is
               bound in open Court to Thomas Lamarr Jun till
               she attaine the age of sixteene years, she
               being ffour years old the fifth day of this
               instant August-

August 1711   HODGES, Charles Ramsey:- Sonn of Thomas Hodges
G 78   by consent of the Mother Charity Hodges and
               this Court is bound to Anne Venman till he at-
               taine the age of 21 years, he being 8 years
               old the Eighteene day of February next, and
               if the said Venman dyes before the said Charles
               attaine the aforsaid age of Twenty one years

then to returne to his Mother Charity Hodges-

August 1715
G 785

HODGES, Elizabeth:- dau of Charity Hodges is bound unto Thomas & Ann Brasheers till she come to the age according to Act of Assembly she being 5 years old the 7 day of May last past, Ann(sic) the said Thomas and Ann Brasheers to learn the said Elizabeth Hodges to read in the Bible-

August 1711
G 77

HODGES, Presosia:- dau of Thomas Hodges by Consent of her Mother Charity Hodges and the Court is bound to Peter Hyett and Anne his wife till She be Sixteene years of Age. She being (blank) years of Age the Thirteenth day of May last-

March 1715
G 719

HODGES, Sarah:- bound to John Carpenter and his assignes till she attaine the age of sixteene yeares or day of marriage being two years old this month-

June 1706
C 74

HOGEN, Mary:- Mary Hogen came into Court & Bound her Daughter Mary Hogen to Henry Neal till age or day of marriage-

November 1703
B 263

HOGES, Thomas:- Sone of Thomas & Charrity Hoges aged 6 years come ye 3d of November next bound to Mr. Richd Pile till 21 years of age ye said Mr. Pile to bring him up to his calleing and to give him 3 years schooleing and if the said Pile Dyeth before ye Ladds age is Expired he is to be bound to noe person Else-

August 1729
P 133

HOLLY, William:- eight years Old the Last day of next february (as tis said) is by the Court here bound to his Godfather William Miles until the said William Holly shall arrive to the age

of twenty one Years Whereupon the said William
Miles in his proper person in Court here Obliges
himself to give his said Godson one Year and a
half Schooling during this Term and at the Expiration thereof to give him a decent Suit of
Apparell and agrees that the Suit of Cloths
shall be made of either drugy or Kersey-

March 1716
H 32

HOLLYDAY, James:- Comes into open Court &
Chooses Leonard Holyday his Guardian the said
James being Nineteen Yeares of Age next June-

November 1744
CC 590

HOLLYDAY, Leonard:- is by the Court here admitted to Choose his Guardian and hereupon he
makes Choice of Doctor Charles Stuart who in
his proper Person in Court here declares his
willingness to accept the same And is by the
same Court approved of on giving such Security
as the Justices of the Court here shall see
Sufficient for the Estate of the aforesaid
Leonard Hollyday-

June 1696
A 9

HOOK, John:- Pet. Blank (sic) Hook wife of
Blank (sic) Hook that John Hook Sonne of
Nathaniell Hook had pursuant to one Agree-
ment made between blank (hook) Mother of the
Said John Hook being one Infant did appeare
to bind out her said Sonne to Thos. Bown-

August 1729
P 133

HOWARD, Sarah:- four years old the last day
of next October (as it is said) is by the
Court here bound to Elizabeth Wildman until
she the said Sarah arrive to the age of Sixteen Years- Whereupon the same Elizabeth in
her proper person in Court here Obliges her-
self to hear the said Sarah to read distinctly
in the bible to Sew with her Needle during
the Term and at the Expiration thereof to give

her a decent Suit of Apparell-

June 1725 L 638	HOWERTON, Jane:- alias Overton aged as tis said 7 years the middle of last December is by the Court here bound to John Orme & Ruth his wife untill she the said Jane arrive to the age of 16 years...to give the girl at the Expiration of her time a decent suit of apparel and to learn her to read before she is free-
June 1736 W 56	HOYE, Mary:- aged as tis said in Court here Fourteen Years last March is by the Justices thereof admitted to Choose her Guardian... Whereupon she makes choice of Thomas Richards of the County afsd Planter who in his proper person in Court here declares his willingness to accept the same-
August 1698 A 332	HOWES, Henry:- sevt to Nathan Veitch adjudged sixteen years...ordered to serve according to Act of Assembly-
March 1721 K 89	HUGHS, William:- Jonathan Waddam by his Petition setts forth to the Court here that he has four years past maintained Willaim (Son of Richard Hughs late of this County) and desires the afd Lad be bound to him, Whereupon the said William is by the Court here bound unto the said Jonathan untill he arrive to the age of Twenty-one years, in Consid^n whereof the said Jonathan oblidges himselfe in Court here to give the said William a years schooling and at the expiration of his time a decent sute of apparell-
June 1711 G 69a	HURST, Mary:- Daughter to Ann Hurst 5 years of age this month of June bound to Ninian Magruder till age ye said Magruder obleidge-

ing himselfe to have ye Child Taught to read
and Sow and Ord^d to Serve accordingly-

August 1735
V 535

HYDE, Ann:- Ordered by the Court that Mary
Medcalfe Widow be allowed 100 pds of Tobacco
Tenn Shillings Current Money...for keeping &
Maintaining-Cloathing a Certain Ann Hyde an
orphan Daughter of Isaac Hyde dec.-

August 1734
V 102

HYDE, Thomas:- an orphan Aged 15 years-the
26 day of next January is by the Court here
bound unto Turner Wootton Gent & his assigns
until he the said Thomas shall arrive to age-
during the term afsd to Learn the said orphan
to read & write as also the art mystery &
Trade of Cordwayner...at Expiration, a Decent
Suit of apparel and at the same time the said
Turner Wootton in his proper person in Court
here promises & agrees that he will not assign
the said Orphan to any Roman Catholick without first Lodging with the Clerk of the Court
here a Writing obligatory in 50 pds current
money...Thomas to be brought up in the relig-
ion Established by Law-

June 1723
L 79

HYNES, Eleanor:- 6 years old last August of
the assent of her Mother in like manner declared is by the Court here bound unto the
sd Francis Piles untill she come to Age...
at expiration of her time a decent suit of
apparel-

June 1723
L 78

HYNES, Elizabeth:- Eleven years old of the
assent of her Mother Jane Hynes declared here
in open Court by the Court here is bound unto
Francis Piles Jun untill she come to age and
the said Francis in his proper person engages
to give the said Eliza. at the Expiration of

her time a decent suit of apparel-

+++++++

March 1750   IRELAND, Alexander:- Aged about Eleven years
LL 134   is By the Court here Bound to Richard White
              till he arrive to the Age of Twenty one years
              and the said Richard White agrees to give
              the said Alexander a year Schooling and the
              customary Freedom Dues at the Expiration of
              his Time of Servitude-

August 1743
CC 3/4

JACKSON, John:- Aged (as tis Said) about thirteen years is by the Court here Bound unto William Wallace untill he the said John Jackson arrive to the age of Twenty one years and the said William Wallace in Court here Promises to Teach or Cause to be taught the said John Jackson during the Term aforesaid to read and Write and at the Expiration thereof to give him a Decent Suit of Apparell-

August 1737
W 497

JAMES:- a Malatto Child of Jane Normans Now Sevt to Richard Keene aged as tis Said Two months is by the court here Sold to Edward Swann of Prince Georges County Planter for Six pounds Two Shillings Current Untill the Sd James Arrive to the age of Twenty one Years-

November 1739
X 496

JAMES, John:- Aged (as tis said) three years ye twenty third Day of this Instant November is by ye Court here Bound unto William Norton until ye sd John Arrives to ye Age of twenty-one Years & ye sd William in Court here promises to do his Endeavour to Learn him during ye term afd to read Distinctly & at ye Expiration thereof to give him a Decent Suit of Apparel-

June 1742
AA 3

JANE:- Ordered by the Court here that Molatto Jane Daughter to Moletto Beck belonging to Samuel Selby aged 12 months the first day of March next to be Bound to Joseph Bladen untill she arrive to the Age of Sixteen years. And ordered Likewise that he be Allowed Three pounds current Money in the next County Levy in Consideration of the sd Molatto Janes Infancy-

August 1711
G 77

JENINGS, James:- Sonn of William Jenings by Consent of his Mother and the Court bound to

Thomas Locker Senr. till he attaine the age
of 18 years, being 2 years old next January-

August 1711
G 77

JENINGS, William:- Sonn of William Jenings
by consent of his Mother Mary Jennings is
bound in open Court to Thomas Locker, Jun.
till he attaine the age of 18 years & being
Nine years old the 27 day of June last-

August 1749
LL 6

JENKINS, Josias:- comes into open Court and
makes choice of John Jenkins as his Guardian
& the said John Jenkins present here in
Court in his proper person declares his Willingness to Accept the same & is admitted
accordingly-

March 1716
H 32

JENKINS, Thomas:- Servt to Notley Rozer adjudged to be Seventeen yeares of Age-
Ordered to Serve According to Act of Assembly-

August 1711
G 77

JENNINGS, Anne:- Daughter of William Jennings
by Consent of her Mother Mary Jennings is
bound to Thomas Locker Sen with consent of
the Court till she attaine the age of 16 years
being 8 years old next September-

June 1718
H 669

JENNINGS, John:- Ordered that John Jennings
Son of Mary Jennings Serve John Hopkins till
he come to age according to Act of Assembly
He being Six years old the Twenty-Sixth day
of Aprill last past. The said Hopkins to give
him a years schooling and a Suite of Cloths
att the Expiration of the said time as also
two white shirts a pair of shoes and stockings and one hatt-

August 1711
G 77

JENNINGS, Sarah:- Daughter of William Jennings
by Consent of her Mother & this Court is bound
to John Dickenson till she attaine the age of
16 years being 5 years old last March and the

said John Dickenson to cause her to be
taught to spinn and Card-

August 1711
G 77

JENNINGS, Thomas:- Sonn of William Jennings
by Consent of his Mother Mary Jennings and
this Court is bound to Edward Broughner till
he attaine the age of 18 years-being 4 years
ole next January-

November 1717
H 310

JOHNSON, John:- by Consent of his Mother
Mary Johnson Comes into open Court and is
bound to Jonathan Wadhams and Joan his wife
for and dureing the Terme of Seven years
from this Day-

November 1728
O 335

JOHNSON, Michael:- aged (as tis said in Court)
fourteen years last September in his proper
person here prays the Justices thereof that
he may be admitted to choose his Guardian
which is granted him whereupon he makes choice
of his Mother Elizabeth Wildman whereupon her
declaring in Court here her Willingness to
accept thereof is admitted accordingly-

June 1716
H 85

JOHNSON, Nathaniel:- Son of Richard Johnson
by Consent of the Court is bound to Evan Jones
and Ann his now wife till he attain the age
of twenty-one yeares he being now six yeares old-

November 1720
K 12

JOHNSON, Nathaniel:- is by the Court here bound
unto William Welsh untill he arrive to the age
of twenty one years, Whereupon the sd William
oblidges himselfe to Instruct and learn the
sd Nathaniel the art and mistery of a Ship-
wright, and to provide for him sufficiently
during the terme-

August 1727
N 491.

JONES, James:- Aged as tis said eighteen years
& Six months this day to wit the twenty-fourth

day of August anno Dm Seventeen hundred &
twenty-Seven comes into court here & on his
prayer is allowed by the Justices thereof to
choose his Guardian whereupon he makes choice
of Thomas Stonestreet & the said Thomas Stonestreet in his proper person in Court here declaring his willingness to undertake the
Guardianship of the said James is by the
Court here admitted thereunto-

June 1714
G 610

JONES, Sophia:- by Consent of her Father in
Law Evan Thomas is bound to Robert Oram and
Ruth his wife till she attaine the Age ac-
cording to Act of Assembly she being four
years of Age the Seaventeene day of Jany last.
The said Robert Oram and Ruth his wife to
teach or cause to be Taught the said Sophia
Jones to read in the Bible-

June 1703
B 239a

JONES, William:- an Orphant Some Years Sence
Left by his parents to one Isaac Williams who
is lately Dead the Lad being 15 years of age
and a halfe By the motion of Mr. Joshua Beall
by way of Petition is hereafter mentioned in
the behalfe of ye orphan Setts fforth...
June ye 22 1703...William Jones made choice
of William Hill his uncle to be his Guardean-

November 1745
DD 279

JOSEPH:- Ordered by the Court here that Mulatto Jane's Male Child named Joseph Aged
(as tis said) three months be bound unto
Richard Keene until he arrive to the Age of
Twenty-one Years and in Consideration of its
Infancy is allowed One thousand pounds of Tobacco in the next County Levy and ordered by
same Court that said Mulatto Jane serve her

Said Master Richard Keene nine Months for
the Trouble of his House and Expences in
keeping said Child to this time-

March 1750
LL 136

JOYCE, Elizah:- Aged about Eleven years the
22d Day of Next April Is by the Court here
Bound unto William Clark untill he arrive
to the Age of Twenty one years and the said
William Clark agres to give him a years Schooling and at the Expiration of the Time of Servitude to have the Accustomed freedom Dues-

January 1700
B 93

JURES, James:- aged 5 years old ye last of
June by his Mother also Jures was bound to
Charles Beall till he arive to one and twenty
years of age- The said Charles Beall is obliged
to Cause him to be taught to wright and read
& to teach him the tread of a carpenter to
finde him all nessasaryes-

June 1698 A 317	KANADY, Daniel:- Servt to Timothy Mohony adjudged to be 11 years of age-
March 1706 C 39	KEEN, Richard:- with ye advice and Consent of his ffriend doe binde himselfe a Servant to Josiah Willson for ye ffull Space and terme of five whole years to doe Such Service or Services as he shall think fitt to Employ him About During the Said Time Except Labouring att ax and hoe and the said Willson doth binde himselfe to find the Said Keen with good Sufficient meal washing Lodging & Desscent apparrell dureing the Said Terme and to Use his Endeveur to Instruct the Said Keen in writeing and acc^{ts} & Learne him & bring him up to Buisiness and at ye Expiration of the said terme ye Said Willson is to give him a Suite Descent apparrell a young horse or Mare & Bridle and Saddle-
August 1698 A 332	KELLY, Bryan:- Servt to John Prather adjudged Fourteen years ordered to serve according to Act of Assembly-
March 1744 CC 276	KELLY, Daniel:- Aged (as tis said) fourteen Years the Twenty nineth Instant is by the Court here bound to Spicer Owen of Prince Georges County Planter and his Assigns until he arrive to the Age of Twenty one years-. And the said Spicer Owen in his proper Person in Court here Promises During the Term aforesaid to Learn the said Daniel Kelly to read and write and at the Expiration of his time of Servitude to give him a Decent Suit of Apparel-
November 1714 G 692	KELLY, James:- Jarvis and Elizabeth Winsor comes into open Court and binds theire Sonn

James Kelly to Timothy Mahaney till he
attaine his age according to Act of Assembly:
he being Eight years of age the fifteenth day
of Aprill next-

August 1698
A 332

KELLY, John:- sevt to John Barrett adjudged fourteen years ordered to serve according to Act of Assembly-

November 1711
G 124

KELLY, Mary:- alis Taylor Daughter of Elizabeth Taylor in open Court is bound to William Coxey and his heires till she come to
the age of Sixteene years being three years
old the Twenty ninth day of May next-

November 1739
X 501

KENNETT, John Boyce:- Aged as it is said in
Court here bound unto Robert Wheeler Senr
until he ye sd John Boyce arrive to ye Age
of Twenty one Years & Daniel Wheeler (Son of
ye sd Robt) in his proper pson in Court here
promises to give ye Boy a Years Schooling
during ye term afd & at ye Expiration thereof to give him a decent Suit of Apparel-

June 1733
S 333

KENNICK, William:- aged (as tis said in Court
here) fifteen years next April in his proper
person prays the Justices thereof that he may
be admitted to Choose his Guardian which is
granted him, Whereupon he makes Choice of John
Brightwell who upon his Declaring in Court
here his Willingness to accept the Same is admitted accordingly and the said John Brightwell in his proper person in Court here obliges
himself to give his said Ward Two years Schooling or to Learn him to Read and Write and afterwards to Bind him to Some handy Craft Trade
untill he arrive to the age of Twenty one years-

March 1711 G 43a	KERMY, Jeremy:- also Macknew two years old ye 11th day of May Last bound to John Barrett till age-
June 1728 O 135	KEY, Elizabeth:- aged (as she says her self) twelve years last May is bound by the Court to John Bradford present here in his proper person until She Arrive to the age of Sixteen Years and the said John Bradford in Court promises During the term af'd to learn the said Elizabeth to read distinctly in the bible not to put her to work at the hoe and at the Expiration of her time to give her a decent Suit of apparel-
August 1698 A 332	KEY, James:- servant to Matthew Mackeboy adjudged Sixteen years ordered to serve according to Act of Assembly-
August 1736 W 150	KEY, James:- Mary Collier in her proper person in Court Bindes her Son James Key aged five years the Seventh Day of next Aprill to Thomas James Jr. until he the said James Key arrive to the age of Twenty one years... and the sd Thomas James in open Court here promises During the Term af'd to Learn the sd James Key to Read and Write and at the Expiration thereof to give him a decent Suit of apparell-
June 1726 L 631,632	KING, Charles:- Aged nine months this day is by the Justices Of the Court here bound unto Jonathan Waddams untill the said Charles King arrive to the Age of 21 years-
March 1713,14 G 539	KING, Elizabeth:- Daughter of Elizabeth King is bound by her Mothers Consent to John Greene or his Assignes till She attaine the age of

Sixteene years being five years of Age this instant March-

August 1711
G 77

KING, John:- Sonn of Edmond King by Consent of his Mother Elizabeth King bound in open Curt to John Henry till he attaine the age of Twenty one years he being ffive years old last Aprill and the said John Henry to learn the sd John King to read well in the Bible-

November 1742
AA 215

KING, Mary:- about four months is by the Court here Bound to William Chesshire and his heirs until She Arrive to the Age of Thirty one Years-

March 1735

KITCHIN, William (see Harding Evans, Page 33.)

June 1710
D 316

KNIGHT, Peter:- Servant to Richd Groome Planter adjudged to be 15 years of Age Ordered ye said Peter Knight Serve ye said Richd Groome according to an Act of Assembly in the Case made & provided-

June 1744
CC 403

LANCASTER, Henry:- Aged (as it is said) Eleven Years on the Twenty fifth of December next is by the Court here bound to Benjamin Chitty until the said Henry Lancaster arrive to the Age of Twenty one years and the said Benjamin Chitty in his proper person in Court here undertakes during the Term aforesaid to Learn the said Henry Lancaster to read and Write and at the Expiration of his time to give him a Suit of Druggett Cloaths a pair of Shoes and Stockings one Castor Hatt and two White Shirts-

January 1705
C 35

LEE, Elizabeth:- Daughter to William Lee borne ye 3d of March 1693 bound to Hugh Ryley till age, ye Said Elizabeth to have 2 years Scooleing-

January 1705
C 35

LEE, Margrett:- borne ye 14th day of January 1695 to (Wilm) Lee bound to Edward (McCunes) till age...to have 2 years Schooleing-

June 1725
L 452

LEECHMAN, Eleanor:- 8 years old the 15 of June instant is by the Court here bound unto Mary Bateman untill she the said Eleanor arrives to the age of 16 years-and the said Mary in her proper person in Court here undertakes to learn the said Eleanor to read during the time afsd and at the Expiration thereof to give her a Decent Suit of Apparel-

June 1725
L 452

LEECHMAN, Samuel:- 11 years old the 15th of June Instant is by the Court here bound unto Mary Bateman untill he arrive to the age of 21 years- and the said Mary in her proper person in Court here undertakes to learn the said Samuel to read during the time afsd and at the Expiration thereof to give him a decent Suit of Aparel-

August 1733 S 402	LEVETT, John:- about Seventeen years LEVETT, Robert:- aged (as tis said) in Court here, about Nineteen years...

in their proper persons pray the Justices
thereof that they may be admitted to Choose
their Guardians which is granted them whereupon they make choice of Edward Sprigg Gent
who upon his declaring in Court here his
Willingness to accept the Same is admitted
accordingly-

June 1745 DD 91	LEVISTON, James:- Aged (as tis said) twelve

years the 7th day of May Last is by the Court
here bound to Michael Dowden of Prince Georges
County Planter until he arrive to the Age of
Twenty One Years and hereupon the said Michael
Dowden in his Proper person in Court here undertakes during the term aforesaid to Learn
the said James Leviston to read and Write
and at the Expiration of his time of Servitude
to give him the freedom dues- Accustomed to
Servants Imported into this Province-

March 1742 AA 341	LEVIT, William:- Ordered by the Court here

that William Levit aged Eight Years as tis
said be Bound to Thomas Morton untill he
arrive to the Age of Twenty Years and the
said Thomas Morton in his proper Person in
Court here Promises to give the said William
Levit Two Years Schooling and at the Expiration of his time a Decent Suit of Apparel-

March 1723 L 243	LEWIS, David:- LEWIS, Jonathan:- Mary Beckett in her proper

person in Court here binds her Sons Jonathan
Lewis & David Lewis both (being twins) Five
years old the 7 of October last unto William

Mordant untill they arrive to the age of 21
years-Whereupon he the said William Mordant
in Court here Engages to Learn the said Jonathan and David to read and write and to give
each of them a decent suit of Apparell at the
Expiration of their time-

June 1715
G 764

LEWIS, John:- Comes into open Court and is
is bound to John Halsall till he Attaine the
Age of Twenty One Years being thirteen years
of Age in January next and to doe his Endeavour to learn him to read and Write-

November 1703
B 262 a

LEWIS, Patience:- By the Consent of her Mother
and John Underwood her ffather in Law 4 years
Old March next Bound to William Conleye &
uxor till age or the day of marriage but in
case of their Deaths to retire to her Mother-

August 1701
B 122

LEWIS, Sarah:- orphant aged nine years the
25th Day of March next was bound to Jeremiah
Snell till 16 years of age or ye Day of
Marriage-

June 1706
C 61

LINZEE, Eliz:- Servt to Mr. Leman adjudged
to be 21 years of Age Ordered that She Serve
According to Act of Assembly in that Case
made and provided-

March 1729
O 411

LLOYD, John:- an Orphan aged (as tis said)
thirteen years or there about is by the Court
here put under the Guardianship of his Kins-
man Samuel Bussey present here in Court in
his proper person who upon declaring in Open
Court his willingness to accept the same is
admitted accordingly and the said Samuel in
like manner promises to give the said Orphan
two Years Schooling during his Minority and

at the Expiration thereof to give her a decent
Suit of Apparell-

March 1729
O 411

LLOYD, Sarah:- an Orphan aged (as tis Said)
three years or thereabouts is by the Court
here put under the Guardianship of her kins-
man James Pelley present here in Court in his
proper person who upon declaring in Open Court
his Willingness to accept the same is admitted
accordingly and the said James in like manner
promises to give the said Orphan two Years
Schooling during her Minority and at the Expiration thereof to give her a decent Suit of Ap-
parell-

March 1735
W 1

LOCKLIN, John:- aged about Two Months is by
the Court here bound unto Samuel Wilson until
he arrive to the age of Twenty-one years and
in consideration of its Infancy the said Samuel is to be allowed fifteen Hundred pounds
of Tobacco in the next County Levy provided
the said John so long live and if he die in
the mean time he the said Samuel is to have
only in proportion to the Time he keeps it
and hereupon Peter Dent and James Boswell
Gent in their proper persons in Court here
undertake that the said Samuel Shall and do
Learn the said John During the Term afd to
Read Distinctly & at the Expiration thereof
to give him a Decent Suit of Apparel-

March 1716
H 32

LONG, Susannah:- Ordered that Susannah Long
Daughter of Benjamin Long Serve Joseph Belt
and his heirs till she Come to Age According
to Act of Assembly She being now Seven Yeares
of Age and the said Joseph Belt or his heirs

to give and deliver unto the said Susannah
Long at the Expiration of her time of Servitude as aforesaid one Suit of Cloaths-

June 1748
HH 169

LOUGHLAN, Henry:- Aged Six Months is by the
Consent of his Mother Priscilla Loughlan and
by the Court bound to William Hitchinson and
Rachel his Wife till he arrives to the age
of Twenty one years and the said William
Hitchinson on his part promises and obliges
himself to learn the said Child to read and
write and at the Expiration of his time to
give him freedom dues according to the Custom
of the Country-

January 1703
B 275

LOVEJOY, Sam[ll]:- Aged 2 years old next May
by Consent of his ffather and Mother was
bound to John Deakins or his assignes till
age-

March 1721
K 83

LOVELACE, Thomas:- an Orphan Boy twelve years
old next June is by Consent of the Court here
bound unto Thomas Wall untill he the said
Orphan arrive to the age of Eighteen years.
Whereupon the said Thomas Wall obliges himselfe to give him at the expiration of his
time a compleat decent Suite of apparell and
a mare bridle and saddle-

June 1710
D 318

LUDWELL, Jane:- orphant of William Ludwell
Deceased being present in Court The Court
appoynted Mr. James Stoddard to be his Guardian ye said Jane being tenn years of age ye
Second day of February last past-

March 1719
H 973

LUKETT, William:- Son of Mary Lukett is by
the Consent of the Court bound to Edward

Offutt and his Assigns till he attain the
age of Twenty one years He being now six
months old-

August 1744   MACCOY, Elizabeth:- Aged (as tis said) Seven
CC 517   Years or thereabouts is by the Court here
               bound to Capt. Charles Higginbottom until she
               Arrive to the Age of Sixteen Years and the
               said Charles Higginbottom in his proper person
               in Court here undertakes to Learn or Cause
               to be Learned the said Elizabeth Maccoy during
               the Term aforesaid to Read, Knitt Spinn, and
               Sew and at the Expiration thereof to give her
               a Decent Suit of Apparel-

August 1744   MACCOY, Henry:- Aged (as tis said) Eleven Years
CC 517   or thereabouts is by the Court here bound to
               Capt. Charles Higginbottom until he Arrives
               to the Age of Twenty one Years And the Said
               Charles Higginbottom in his proper person in
               Court here undertakes to learn the said Henry
               Maccoy during the Term aforesaid to Read and
               Writ and at the Expiration thereof to give
               him a Decent Suit of Apparel-

August 1736   MACDONALD, Groves:- Grace Macdonald in her
W 150   proper person in Court here binds her Son
               Groves Macdonald aged Two Years the twenty
               Sixth day of May last to Matthew Markland un-
               til he the sd Groves Arrives to the age of
               Twenty one years and the sd Matthew in open
               Court here promises During the Term afsd to
               Learn the sd Groves to Read and Write & at
               the Expiration thereof to give him a Decent
               suit of apparell-

August 1698   MACE, Henry:- servt to Captaine Edward Brocke
A 332   adjudged twenty years-ordered to serve accord-
               ing to act of assembly-

June 1717   MACKDONALD, Robert:- Aged ffive years next
H 243   Christmas, and

MACKDONALD, Susannah:- Twelve Months this Day
are by Consent of this Court bound to John
Hawkins and his heirs till they Severally
Attain their Age-

November 1698
A 355

MACKEBOY, William:- servant to Mr. John Smith
adjudged to be 14 years old- to serve according to Act of Assembly-

March 1728
O 13

MACKUNE, Edward:- (an orphan) Aged as tis said
about fifteen Years comes into Court here in
his proper person and prays he may be admitted
to Choose his Guardian-which is granted, Whereupon he makes Choice of Edward Marler who upon
his declaring in Court here his willingness
to accept the same is admitted accordingly-

March 1728
O 13

MACKUNE, William:- (aged as tis said) twelve
years Sometimes last August present here in
Court is bound to his Uncle Ralph Marler from
this time for Seven Years and the said Ralph
in his proper person in Court here Engages to
use his Endeavour to Learn his nephew the
Carpenters trade and at the Expiration of his
time to give him a decent Suit of Apparel-

November 1724
L 376

MACMILLION, John:- 3 yrs old the last day of
October last is by the Court here bound unto
John Hawkins untill the sd John Macmillion
arrive to the age of 21 - agreement, to give
ye sd lad a years schooling and at ye Expiration a decent Suit of apparell-

June 1743
AA 478

MAGRUDER, Elias:- Samuel Magruder Sen is by
the Court here appointed Guardian to Elias
Magruder his Son and Declares his Willingness
to accept the Same-

June 1737 W 417	MAGRUDER, George:- aged as it is said in Court here Fifteen Years or thereabouts is by the Justices thereof admitted to Choose his guardian Whereupon he makes Choice of Robert Whitaker of the County af'd Gent. Who in his proper person in Court Declares his Willingness to accept the same-
March 1745 DD 9	MAGRUDER, Susanah:- is by the Court here admitted to Choose her Guardian and hereupon She makes Choice of George Magruder of Prince Georges County Planter who in his Proper person in Court here declares his Willingness to accept the Same-
November 1738 X 192	MALE CHILD:- Mallatto Jane's Male Child being now Two Months old is by the Court here Bound unto Walter Brooke Gent until it Arrive to Age of twenty-one years & in Consid^n of Two pounds Tenn Shillings Currt Money Allowed him the sd Walter in the next County Levy he promises during the Term af'd to give the Said Child a years Schooling & at the Expiration thereof a Decent Suit of Apparel-
March 1750 LL 134	MANDUIT, Jasper:- aged 17 years next July in Open Court makes Choice of Alexander Jackson as his Guardian who in his proper person in Court Accepts the same-
November 1748 KK 34	MANEY, Jemima:- Aged (as it is said) 16 months is by the Court here bound to John Beall son of Robert until she arrive to the age of 16- agreement, to learn the said Jemima to Read and at Expiration of her time of servitude to give her freedom dues according to the Custom of this Country-

August 1698 MARONEY, James:- servt to John Barrott
A 332   adjudged seventeen years- ordered to serve
             according to Act of Assembly-

November 1735 MARSHALL, William:- aged as it is Said in
V 620   Court here Fifteen Years or thereabouts is
               by the Court here admitted to choose his
               Guardian Whereupon he makes choice of his
               Brother Thomas Marshall Jun of Prince Georges
               County planter who Declares his Willing-
               ness to accept-

November 1742 MARY:- Ordered by the Court here that Mo-
AA 192   latto Cates Bastard Child named Mary Aged
               about Nine months be Bound to Doctor John
               Haswell untill she arrive to age of Sixteen
               years-

June 1718   MAUNDER, Ann:- Ordered that Ann Maunder
H 670   Daughter of William Maunder decd Serve John
            Hopkins till she Comes to Age according to
            Act of Assembly. She being five years old
            the Eighth day of September next and to Give
            the said Ann Maunder Six Months Schooling
            And a Suite of apparell at the expiration of
            the Terme aforementioned & c.

June 1721   MEARES, Isaac:- about five years
K 245   MEARES, James:- about twelve years old
            MEARES, William:- about Eight years, are by
            the Consent of their Mother Martha Meares now
            here Certified in Court under her hand bound
            by the same Court unto Joseph West his heirs
            and assigns untill they respectively arrive
            to the age of Twenty-one years- Whereupon the
            said Joseph West Undertakes in his proper per-
            son in Court here to learn & instruct the

Severall Minors to read distinctly in the
bible, and at the expiration of their severall termes to give each of them a decent
suite of apparell-

March 1738
W 652

MERRETT, Mary:- aged Eleven years next October of ye consent of her Mother Sarah Merrett Certified by Peter Dent Gent one of the
Justices of the Court here is by ye same Court
bound Unto Oliver Harris until She Arrive to
ye Age of Sixteen Years. Whereupon he promises
in Court here to give her During ye Term af^d
a Years Schooling to Learn her to Spinn & Knit
& at the Expiration thereof to give her a
Decent Suit of Apparell-

August 1703
B 251

MILES, Mary:- (and Luke Barnett) Nathaniell
Wickham & Samuell Brasheer Planters of Prince
Georges stand justly indebted unto Luke Bar-
nett & Mary Miles orphant children of Thomas
Barnett Lately Deceased- in the full & just
Sume of 22 pds-8 pence Sterling-

June 1745
DD 89

MILLER, Robert:- Aged (as tis said) Eight
Years is by the Court here bound unto Robert
Gordon of Prince Georges County Planter until
he Arrives to the Age of Twenty one Years-
And hereupon the said Robert Gordon in Consideration thereof undertakes During the term
aforesaid to give the same Robert Miller one
years Schooling and at Expiration of his time
of Servitude to give him what is Allowed by
Law to Servants Imported into this Country-

August 1714
G 633

MILLS, Catherine:- Daughter of William Mills
by Consent of the Court bound to Nathan Magruder and his heires till She attaine her

Age according to act of Assembly She being
(----) and to have a years Schooleing and
Suite of Cloathes of Serge or (Shiffe) when
free-

| March 1708
C 221a | MILLS, Tabitha:- born ye 26th of October 1697
MILLS, Verlinda:-borne ye 7th day of Jan 1699
MILLS, William:-borne ye 11th day of October
    1695. (The Ages of Wm. Mills Children) |

| March 1723
L 4 | MIRA, Alicia:- will be 5 yrs old next May
MIRA, Anna Christianna:-will be 7 yrs old
        next August,
MIRA, Hans Peter:-will be 3 yrs old next April,
        Reverend Jacob Henderson produces to the
Court here Servants to be adjudged of their
ages namely Anna Christianna Mira, Alicia
Mira, Hans Peter Mira- |

| June 1748
HH 176 | MITCHEL, Lydia:- aged about nine Years is by
the Court here bound to Katherine Pritchard
till She arrives to the age of Sixteen Years
and the said Katherine promises and obliges
herself to learn or cause the said Lydia to
be learned to Read Sew Spin & Knit and at the
Expiration of her time to give her freedom
dues according to the Custom of the Country- |

| November 1703
B 262a | MORRIS, Richard:- Servant to James Beall ad-
judged to be 12 years of age-ordered he serve
according to an Act of Assembly in that Case
made and provided- |

| March 1721
K 83 | MORRISS, Mary:- an Infant being about Two Years
old at this time is by the Court here bound
unto George Shirley untill she arrive to the
age of Sixteen years, Provided nevertheless |

that if Hannah Price Mother of the said Mary
and Servt of the Said George do Serve her said
Master one year besides her Indented time now
and to him, That then the said Child is to be
free, the said George oblidging himselfe to
find the said Mary all necessarys during the
time afsd-

March 1723
L 241

MULVAINE, Eleanor:- 4 years old the 31 of
December 1715 is by the Court here bound unto
James Perrie untill She Come to the age of 16
years whereupon the said James Ingages in Court
here to Learn the said Eleanor to Read, not
to let her work at the hoe during her time of
Service and at the Expiration thereof to give
her a decent Suit of Apparel-

March 1723
L 2

NASH, John:- aged 6 years the 4th day of May
next is by ye Court here bound to Robert Coots
and Mary his Wife untill the said John Nash
arrive to the age of 21 years & the said Robert
in Court here oblidges himself to Learn the
Lad to read distinctly in the Bible And at the
Expiration of his time to give him a decent
suit of Apparel-

March 1733
S 249,250

NAVANE, James:- an Orphan Aged as tis said
in Court here Eleven years next June by same
Court is bound unto Daniel Carroll of Upper
Marlborough until he the said James shall arrive to age and the said Daniel present here
in Court in his proper person promises to
Learn the said Orphan during the time afsd
to Read and Write and at the Expiration thereof to give him a Decent Suit of Apparell-

March 1740
X 571

NEALL, Jane:- Ordered by ye Court here ye Petr.
Oliver Roe be allowed in ye next County Levy
Six Pounds Current Money for his Trouble &
Expense-...ye Child named Jane Neall two Years
Old ye Eighteenth of this March Instant is by
ye Court here bound to ye petr. until she Arrive to ye Age of Sixteen years. Whereupon he
promises to learne her to Read during ye term
afsd & at ye Expiration thereof to give her
a Decent Suit of Apparel-

March 1746
DD 403

NEALE, Richard:- is by the Court here admitted
to Choose his Guardian and hereupon he makes
Choice of Joseph Selby of Prince Georges County
Planter who in his Proper Person in Court here
declares his Willingness to Accept the Same
And it is ordered by the same Court that the

said Joseph Selby take the Effects of the
said Neale Into his Possession from the
Administratrix of Arthur Neale deceased-

November 1738
X 192

NICHOLLS, Mary:- Daughter of Grace Nicholls
is by the Court here Bound to Mary White until
she Arrive to age & in Consid^n of Two pounds
Tenn Shillings Current Money Allowed her the
sd Mary White in the next County Levy...She
promises in Court here to Learn the sd Mary
Nicholls during the Term afd to read distinctly in the Bible & at the Expiration thereof to give her a Decent Suit of apparel-

June 1724
L 312

NICHOLLS, Son of Wm.:- Henry Fitch by his
petition sets forth to the Court here that a
certain Wm. Clarke of Prince Georges County
having intermarried with Anne the Widow and
adx of Wm. Nicholls lately decd. who left be-
hind him a Son now about Six years old-

March 1728
O 14

NICHOLLS, William:- (an Orphan) aged as tis
said about fifteen years comes into Court
here in his proper person and prays he may
be admitted to Choose his Guardian which is
Granted- Whereupon he makes choice of his
uncle Brock MockBoy who upon his declaring
in Court here his Willingness to accept the
same is admitted accordingly-

June 1716
H 85

NORMAN, Ann:- Daughter of Mary Taylor is bound
to Michael and Elizabeth Wellman till she Coem
to age according to Act of Assembly being five
Years old the 25th of January last-

March 1711
G 43

NORMAN, Rebecka:- Daughter to Eliz. Norman now
Eliz. Taylor aged 4 years old next November
bound to Nath^{ll} Wickham till age or Day of
Marriage-

August 1698   NORTON, Henry:- servt to Jonathan Simons
A 332   adjudged twenty years ordered to serve
                 according to act of Assembly-

November 1700   ONEBEY, Thomas:- Sonn of Stephen Onebey
B 81   came & Desiered James Watts his Father
                 in Law to be his Guardian which was al-
                 lowed by ye Court & c.,-

June 1725   OVERTON, Jane:- (see Howerton, Jane, p.53)

November 1716 H 138	PAGGETT, William:- Comes into open Court and chooses Thomas Paggett for his Guardian-
November 1696 A 57	PAINE, James:- Sonn of John Paine about Seaven years old by his fathers Consent is bound to serve Samuell Westley untill he arrives to 21 yeares-
November 1721 K 421	PALLE, Anna:- William & Jane Vinicum by their Petition set forth to this Court here that they have had in their Possession to Maintain one Orphan Girl named Anna Palle Daughter of Reb^a Taylor & in Consideration for satisfaction the Mother afd hath give them an obligation that her Daughter should be bound to them according to the Custom of the Court in such Cases the girl being at Decemb^r about the Twenty fifth Twelve years of age- Request granted-
November 1721 K 417	PALLY, James:- aged Six Years the Last day of March Last is by the Court here bound unto William Wofford Jun till he arrive to Twenty-one years the said William Wofford Oblidging himself in Court here to give the said James one years Schooling when he is Twelve years Old and a Decent Suit of Apparel at the Expiration of his Time-
June 1698 A 317	PATRICK, Richard:- Servt to Henry Gutridge adj. to be 17 years-
June 1737 W 419	PAYNE, Moses:- Rachel Payne in her proper person in Court here binds her Son Moses Payne Two Years old last November as tis now Said unto John Lowe until he the Sd Moses Arrive to the age of Twenty one Years & the Sd John in Court here promises that During the Term afd he Will Learn the sd Moses Payne to Read &

at the Expiration thereof give him a Decent
Suit of Apparel-

November 1749   PECK, John:- Son of Jane Peck aged about 15
LL 80   Months by Court bound unto Thomas Contee un-
                 till he the said John Shall arrive to the Age
                 of 21 years-agreement, at the Expiration of
                 his time of Servitude, freedom Dues accord-
                 ing to the custom of the County-

November 1744   PECK, Joseph:- the Son of Mullatto Jane aged
CC 585   (as tis said) Tenn Months is by the Court here
                 bound to William Beanes Jun of Prince Georges
                 County Gent until he Arrive to the Age of
                 Twenty-one Years and the said William Beanes
                 Jun in his Proper Person in Court here under-
                 takes to Give the said Joseph Peck during the
                 Term aforesaid one Years Schooling and at the
                 Expiration thereof the Usual freedom Dues-

November 1732   PERRIE, Samuel:- aged (as tis said in Court
S 119   here) almost nineteen years in his proper
                 person prays the Justices thereof that he
                 may be admitted to Choose his Guardian which
                 is granted him, Whereupon he makes Choice of
                 Capt. Charles Somerset Smith who upon his
                 declaring in Court here his willingness to
                 accept the same is admitted accordingly-

November 1725   PERRY, Benjamin:- aged 15 yrs the 10th day of
L 511   next May (as tis said) comes into Court here
                 in his proper person and on his Prayer is al-
                 lowed by the Court here to Choose his Guardian.
                 Whereupon he makes choice of his Brother Charles
                 Perry of the County afd and he the said Charles
                 in his proper person in Court here declaring
                 his willingness to undertake the Guardianship

of the said Benjamin is by the Justices of
the Court here admitted thereunto-

June 1725
L 453

PERRY, James:- Son of Joseph Perry deceased
and of Elizabeth now wife of John Anderson,
Tailor, 16 years old the 1st day of March
last into Court here in his proper person
comes and prays he may be admitted to choose
his Guardian and being so admitted he in
Court here chooses his Brother Charles Perry
for his Guardian and the said Charles in
Court here declares his willingness to accept
the Guardianship-

March 1697
A 296

PERRY, John:- the Sonn of Susannah Perry
being four years old next August by the consent of his Mother bound unto George Prater
until he arrives unto 21 yeares of age-said
Prater to doe his Endeavour to Learne the
said Child to Read and write & at the Expiration of his time to give him two Suites of
apparrell the one Keirsey the other Serge
with two of a Sort of all other necessary
apparrell-

November 1738
X 189

PICKETTS, Amy:- aged as tis Said one year the
Seventh day of Last March is by the Court here
Bound to William Osburn until She arrive to
age Whereupon he agrees in Court here to give
the sd Amy During the Term afd one Years
Schooling & at the Expiration thereof a Decent
Suit of Apparell-

November 1735
V 617

PILES, Hunter:- aged (as is Said) 16 years or
thereabouts, present herein in Court in his proper person be admitted to Choose his Guardian,
whereupon he makes Choice of Leonard Piles of

Prince Georges County Planter who in his
proper person in Court here Declares his
Willingness to accept the same-

June 1743
AA 676

PILES, Richard:- (as tis said) Sixteen
years last February, and
PILES, William:- (as tis said) fourteen
Years last Aprill is by the Court here admitted to Choose their Guardian and hereupon they make Choice of George Parker of
Prince Georges County-Gent who in his proper
person in Court here declares his willingness
to accept the Same-

November 1748
KK 26

PLASAY, Mary:- a minor aged about 16 years in
her proper person in Court here Makes choice
of Catherine Plasay her Mother for her Guardian who by Letter to this Court Declares her
willingness to Accept of that Trust-

August 1743
CC 4

POTTENGER, Prisella:- Aged (as tis said) fif-
teen Years is by the Court here Admitted to
Chuse her Guardian and hereupon she makes
Choice of James Mullican of Prince Georges
County Planter who in his proper Person in
Court here declares his willingness to accept
the same-

March 1745
DD 19

POTTENGER, Samuel:- is by the Court here admitted to Choose his Guardian and hereupon he
makes Choice of James Draine of Prince Georges
County Planter who in his proper person in
Court here Declares his Willingness to Accept
the Same-

August 1747
CG 97

POTTINGER, Robert:- aged fourteen years makes
Choice of James Draine of Prince Georges
County planter for his Guardian who in his
proper person in Court here accepts that Trust-

June 1735
V 401

POTTINGER, Sarah:- Aged as it is Said in
Court here Fifteen years the Eighth Day of
Last May is by the Court here admitted to
Choose her Guardian Whereupon She makes
Choice of Zephiniah Wade who in his proper
Person in Court here Declares his willing=
ness to accept the same-

August 1726
N 8

PRATHER, Aaron:- of a competent age as tis
said to wit of about fifteen years comes
into Court here in his proper person and on
his prayer is allow^d by the Court here to
Choose his Guardian whereupon he makes Choice
of Thomas Williams and the said Thomas Williams in his proper person also in Court here
declaring his willingness to undertake the
Guardianship of the said Minor is by the
Court here admitted thereunto-

March 1742
AA 351

PRINCE, Mary:- Ordered by the Court here
that Mary Prince Aged Two years the Seventh
day of April be bound to Humphry Whitemore
untill she Arrives to the Age of Sixteen
Years and the said Humphry Whitemore in his
Proper Person in Court here Promises to give
the said Mary Prince a decent Suit of Apparel
at the Expiration of her time-

June 1726
L 638

PRINDWELL, John:- Aged 14 years the 29 of next
September (at the request of Benjamin Attien
who married his sister as well as of his own
consent) is bound to Captain Leonard Hollyday
untill the said John arrive to the age of twenty
years...agreement, to give the said John at the
Expiration of his time a decent suit of Broad-

cloth and not to imploy the said lad during
the time af'd at the axe or hoe, and that in
case of Capt Hollydays death before the said
John is free it is then to be in the lads
Election either to be bound out anew or remain with the Extx or the Admx of Capt.
Hollyday-

June 1747
FF 620

PRISCILLA:- Ordered by the Court here that
Priscilla the Daughter of Jane Peek aged as
it is said about Eight months be bound unto
Robert Richards and his wife Edith for the
Term of Fifteen years and four months in Consideration of which the said Robert and Edith
promise and oblidge themselves to learn or
Cause the said Priscilla to be Learned to
read to spin to Knit & to sew and at the Expiration of her Servitude to give her freedom
Dues agreeable to the Custom of the Country-

August 1737
W 499

PUMFREY, William:- Aged as tis Said in Court
here four years the Tenth Day of Last January
is by the Court here Bound to Samuel Waters
Senior Until the sd William Shall Arrive to
the Age of Twenty-one years-Whereupon the Sd
Samuel in Court here promises During the Term
af'd to Learn the Said Lad to Read & Write- at
the Expiration thereof to give him a Decent
Suit of Apparell-

March 1703
B 232

PUNCH, Page:- Son of Mary Punch tenn years
old the 13th Day of Decr past by the consent
of his Mother was bound to Mr. Clement Brooke
till he arive to ye age of one and twenty-

June 1745
DD 89

QUEEN, James:- Aged (as tis said) Sixteen
Years in January last is by the Court here
admitted to Choose his Guardian and hereupon he makes Choice of William Pritchett of
Prince Georges County Planter who in his
proper person in Court here declares his
Willingness to Accept the Same-

March 1732
R 402

RACHEL:- Elizabeth Grimes bastard child being named Rachel is by the Court here bound unto the said Edward Willett until it shall arrive to the age of Sixteen years...& the said Elizabeth Grimes is dismist-

November 1699
B 1a

RAWLINGS, Jo^n:- Ordered Jo^n Rawlings ye Sone of Wm. Rawlings being seven years of age serve Collon^{ll} Jo^n Addison untill he arrive to ye age of twenty-one years-

November 1728
O 331

RAY, Anne:- aged Six years the twenty-eighth day of March next is by the Court here bound to Stephen Hampton until she arrive to age and the said Stephen in his proper person in Court here promises to give the said Anne at the Expiration of her time a decent Suit of Apparell...and during the term afsd to learn her to read (See Thomas Birdwhistle, page 9)

March 1739
X 277

RAY, James:- Born (as tis said) ye first Day of October One Thousand Seven Hundred-Twenty-ffive is by ye Court here bound to Samuel Busey until he ye said James Arive to ye Age of Twenty one years and ye sd Samuel Busey in Court here promises to learn him during ye Term af'd to Read & write & at ye Expiracon thereof to give him a Decent Suit of Apparel-

August 1730
P 454

REYNER, James:- (Son of Sarah Reyner) aged thirteen Months is by the Court here bound to Charles Davis until he shall come to age & the said Charles Davis in his proper person in Court here promises to learn the said James to read during the term afsd & at the Expiration thereof to give him a Decent Suit of Apparell-

November 1750 RIGBY, Thomas:- Upon a motion made by Henry
LL 244   Wilsford & Mary his Wife, they are by the
               Court here Appointed Guardian to Thomas Rigby
               a Minor of the Age of 8 years-

June 1697   RISTON, Edward:- Abigall Clifford in open
A 170   court binds her child called Edward Riston
               unto Peter Skamper until 21-said child now
               being three years old-Said Peter Scampers in
               open Court doth acknowledge that he will
               learne the said child to Reade & write...at
               Expiration give him two Suits of Cloaths ye
               one Kersey, the other Serge with two of a
               sort of all other necessary apparell-

March 1721   ROBENSON, Andrew:- On the Petition of Cath-
K 102   erine Robinson setting forth to the Court
               here she formerly bound her son Andrew Rob-
               enson to George Gentle in order to learn his
               trade, And that the said George has neglected
               to comply with that, but instead thereof suf-
               fers him to pursue very vitious courses which
               may be in time of fatall consequence to the
               boy, It was adjudged by the same Court That
               the said Andrew be removed from the apprentice-
               shipp of the said George Gentle and bound the
               remaining part of his time unto John Middleton,
               in consideration of him the said John Middle-
               ton paying twelve hundred pounds of tob^a to
               the said Gentle, which the said John in Court
               here in his proper person undertooke to doe,
               As also to give the said Andrew a years school-
               ing and at the expiration of his time a good
               decent Suite of apparell-

March 1735 V 302	ROBERTS, Elizabeth:- Aged Two Years and Three months the 25 day of this Instant March is by the Court here bound Unto James Read Until She Arrives to Age-Whereupon Christopher Ellis of Prince Georges County Planter in his proper person in Court here Obliges himself That the afsd James Read Shall Well & Truly During the Term afd Learn the said Elizabeth to Read Distinctly in the Bible & at the Expiration thereof give her a Decent Suit of Apparel-
August 1711 G 78	ROBESON, Andrew:- five years old last May, and ROBESON, Charles:- tenn years old January last past...Sonns of Andrew Robeson by Consent of theire Mother Catherine Robeson and this Court is bound to George Gentell till they Severally attaine the age of Twenty-one years. The said George Gentell to doe his Endeavour to learn them the Trade of a Carpenter-
November 1919 H 929	ROBINS, John:- Aged nine years is by consent of the Court bound to John Queen or his assigns till he come to age, the said John Queen to give him one years schooling and a compleat suite of apparell at the expiration of his time-
November 1719 H 929	ROBINS, William:- bound to James Robins by Consent of this Court till he comes to age, the said James Robins to give him a years schooling and a compleat sute of apparell at the end of his time, the said William Robins being now eight years of age-
June 1710 D 316a	ROBINSON, William:- Servant to Samuel Magruder Jr. adjudged to be 11 years of age ordered ye

said William Robinson Serve ye said Samuell
Magruder according to an Act of Assembly in
Case made & provided-

June 1717
H 240

ROGERS, Elizabeth:- is by Consent of the Court
bound to John Brent and Elizabeth his wife
and their Heirs till age According to Act of
Assembly. Elizabeth Rogers five weeks old
this Day. The said John Brent allowed for
keeping the young Child Twelve hundred pounds
of Tobacco next Levy Court and Eight Hundred
the year after-(See Margaret Hall, page 46)

June 1717
H 241

ROGERS, Mary:- Two Years and an half, and
ROGERS, William:- being Eight years old this
Day are by consent of this Court bound to
John Wight and his Wife their heirs and As-
signes till they Severally Attain their ages
According to Act of Assembly-the said Wight
to do his endeavour to learn them to read in
the Bible-

November 1696
A 57

ROSS, Alexander:- Servt to Phillip Gittings
adjudged to be 15 years of age & to serve
according to Act of Assembly-

June 1727
N 350

ROZER, Anne:- (Daughter of Mr. Notley Rozer
decd) of about Sixteen years of age (as tis
said) comes into Court here & on her prayer
is allowed by the Justices here to Choose her
Guardian-whereupon she makes Choice of her
uncle Mr. William Digges Gent & the said William in his proper person in Court here declaring his willingness to undertake the
Guardianship of the Said Anne is by the Court
here admitted thereunto-

August 1724
L 333

RYNE, Richard:- a poor Motherless boy 8 yrs
old 20 day of last June is by the Justices
of this Court here bound unto Joanna Edgar
widow untill he Arrive to the age of 21
years-said Joanna undertakes to learn the
said Lad to read distinctly in the Bible
and at Expiration to give him a Decent Suit
of Kersey Cloaths-

November 1707 C 180	SAFFORNS, Mary:- Daughter to James & Mary Safforne 5 years of age bound to Duke Scott and his wife till age-
November 1738 X 192	SAMUEL:- Mary Wedges Malatto Child Born the Thirty first day of October Last is by the Court here bound unto Thomas Harwood until it Arrive to the age of Thirty one years & in Consideration of its infancy the sd Thomas Harwood is allowed...in the Next County Levy fifteen Shillings Current Money-
June 1740 X 661,662	SARAH:- Catherine Graham's Child named Sarah (two months Old) be a Servt until it Arive to the Age of Thirty one years by ye Court here adjudged according to Act of Assembly in such cases made & Provided. And hereupon ye Child afd is bound unto John Clagett of Rock Creek of Prince Georges County Planter until it arrive to ye afd Age of Thirty one Years & ye sd John in Court promises at ye Expiration of ye time to Give her a decent Suit of Apparel-
November 1711 G 125	SARAH:- Ordered that the Mallatto Girle called Sarah borne of the body of Elizabeth Taylor Serve James Gibbs till she attaine the age of thirty one years being now ffive months old To serve him the said Gibbs his heires or Assignes during the Terme aforesaid he or they paying the sume of Six hundred and fifty pounds of Tob[a] for the said Girle to and for the use of Prince Georges County-
March 1745 DD 16	SELBY, John:- is by the Court here admitted to Choose his Guardian and hereupon he makes

Choice of Samuel Selby of Prince Georges
County Planter who in his proper person in
Court here declares his Willingness to Accept
the same-

March 1745 SELBY, Sarah:- is by the Court here admitted
DD 16   to choose her Guardian and hereupon she makes
             Choice of Samuel Selby of Prince Georges County
             Planter who in his proper person in Court here
             declares his Willingness to Accept the Same-

March 1745 SELBY, Susanah:- is by the Court here admitted
DD 20   to Choose her Guardian and hereupon she makes
             Choice of Thomas Selby of Prince Georges County
             Planter who in his Proper person in Court here
             declares his willingness to accept the Same-

March 1696/7 SESELL, John:- aged 7 years the 24 of December
A 146   Last past, and
             SESELL, Phillip:- aged 5 yeares the 28 day
             of this Instant, and
             SESELL, Susan:- aged 2 yeares 3d of January Last.
             "I, William Sesell by the Request of my
             wife as she lay upon her death bed, I have dis-
             posed of my children to Marreen Devall and his
             heires till they are of age- Request your Wor-
             ships to bind these children this Court to
             the aforesaid Devall and his heires to the age
             of 21; and the girle att 16-March 19, 1697"

March 1713/14 SEYMOUR, Elizabeth:- by Consent of her Mother
G 539   Elizabeth Baley comes into Court and is bound
             unto William Hunter or his assignes till she
             Attaine the age of Sixteene years according
             to act of Assembly She being three years and

a half old the first day of this instant Mar-

June 1696
A 9

SHAW, Mary:- dau of John Shaw aged three years
or thereabouts bound out to Thomas Brooke Esq.
according to Act of Assembly-

June 1725
L 452

SHEPPARD, Ann:- Ruth Sheppards child named
Ann Sheppard 2 years old the 10 day of June
instant is by the Court here bound to Richard
Croxall until she the said Ann come to the
Age of 16 years- and in Consideration of the
Childs Infancy the said Richard is to be allowed 700 pds of Tobacco In the next County
Levy and hereupon the said Richard in his
proper person in Court here undertakes to
learn the said Anne to read during the time
afd and at the end thereof to give her a decent suit of Apparel-

March 1747
GG 458

SHIRLY, Ann:- James Oram and Mary his wife
by Consent of the Court here do bind unto
William Cumming Esquire of Ann Arundel County
and Margaret his Wife, Ann Shirly (Aged ten
Years the twenty fifth day of February last
past) the Daughter of said Mary Oram until
She arrives to the Age of Sixteen Years in
Consideration of which the said William
Cumming on the part of himself and Wife
promises to give the said Ann a years Schooling and at the Expiration of her time of
Servitude freedom dues Agreeable to the Custom of the Country-

September 1701
B 137

SHUNNAM, John:- Servant to John Lewis adjudged
to be 15 years of Age-Ordered that he Serve
his Said Master according to Law-

August 1729 P 135	SILKWOOD (Male child):- Margaret Silkwoods bastard Child (being a male) born the first day of April last is by the Court here bound unto William Davis afsd until the said Child arrive to the age of Twenty one Years and the said William Davis in his proper person in Court here Promises that during the term afsd he will Learn the said child to read (if he has an opportunity) and at the Expiration thereof to give it a decent Suit of Apparell in Consideration of which and the Childs Infancy the said William Davis is to be allowed in the next County Levy Six hundred pounds of Tobacco-
June 1743 AA 476	SIMMS, Cleyburn:- Aged (as tis said) thirteen years the Eighth day of April last is by the Court here admitted to Choose his Guardian and hereupon he makes Choice of his Father Cleyburn Simms of Prince Georges County Planter who in Court here declares his Willingness to accept the same-
August 1728 O 234	SKINNER, Mackall:- (aged as tis said in Court) twenty years last January in his proper person here prays the Justices that he may be admitted to Choose his guardian which is granted him whereupon he makes Choice of his Brother Robert Skinner who upon his declaring in Court here his Willingness to accept the same is admitted Accordingly-
August 1728 O 235	SKINNER, Nathaniel:- (aged as tis said in Court) Seventeen Years last april in his proper person here prays the Justices that he may be admitted

to Choose his guardian which is granted him
whereupon he makes Choice of his Brother
Robert Skinner who upon his declaring in
Court here his Willingness to accept the
Same is admitted accordingly-

November 1725
L 507

SMART, Bartholomew:- 12 years old next Jan=
uary is by the Court here bound to Thomas
Wall untill he the said Bartholomew arrive
to the age of 20 yrs- and in consideration
of the said Lad being so afd bound he is to
have during the time afd bound he is to have
during the time afd 1 years Schooling and
at Expiration of the time a Decent suit of
Apparell-

March 1705
B 352c

SMITH, Daniell:- Sone of Danll Smith Deceased by the consent of Dorothy Owen his
Mother aged nine years of age ye 10th day of
June next bound to Mr. Joshua Cecell till he
arrives to ye age of 21 in consideration
whereof the Said Joshua Cecell obliedges himselfe or his assignes to Endeavour in two
years to have the said Dan^a Taught to wright
and read and at Ye Expiration of ye said
terme of years to Lett him have well cloathd
to ye value of 5 pds sterling-

June 1748
HH 178

SMOOT, John:- aged Sixteen Years in Court
here makes Choice of George Bussy Junior for
his Guardian who declares his Willingness
to Accept of that Trust-

August 1714
G 633

SPARROW, Mary:- Daughter of William Sparrow
is by Consent of the Court bound to Edward *
Willett and his heires till she Come to Age

according to Act of Assembly She being two
yeares old the Twelfth day of March last-

June 1736
W 51

SPENCER, Joseph:- aged as tis said in Court
here Eleven Years the first day of October
next is by the Justices thereof bound unto
the Petr. (John Dunn) until he shall Arrive
to the Age of Twenty one years & the sd
John Dunn in Court here promises to Learn the
sd Joseph Spencer during the Term afsd to
Read & write & at the Expiration thereof to
give him a decent Suit of apparel-

June 1737
W 423

SPRIGG, Edward:- Aged as it is Said in Court
here Sixteen years or thereabouts is by the
Justices thereof admitted to Choose his guardian Whereupon he makes Choice of his Brother
Thomas Sprigg of the County afd Gent Who in
his proper person in Court here Declares his
Willingness to accept the Same-

November 1736
W 266

SPRIGG, John:- aged as Tis Said in Court here
Twenty Years or thereabouts is by the Justices
thereof Admitted to Choose his Guardian Whereupon he makes Choice of his Brother Thomas
Sprigg of Prince Georges County Gent who in
his proper person in Court here Declares his
Willingness to Accept ye Same-

March 1697
A 298

STEVENS, Edward:- Mr. William Hatton desiers
an Orphant Child Left to his Care by the parents thereof being 7 years old in December
Last named Edward Stevens be bound to him according to the custom of the court...bound
untill 21...said Hatton to doe his Endeavour
to Learne the Lad to Reade & write and at Ex-

piration 2 suits of cloaths, the one Keirsey-
the other Serge & 2 of a sort of all other
necessary apparrell & c.

June 1711   STEWART, Elinor:- an Orph^t of Margery Steward
G 69   three years of Age ye 25th day of January
                   next bound to John ffergison till Age-

November 1744   STIMPSON, Benjamin:- is by the Court here
CC 585   Admitted to Choose his Guardian And hereupon
                   he makes Choice of George Hardy Sen of Prince
                   Georges County Planter who in his proper per-
                   son in Court here declares his willingness
                   to accept the same-

August 1743   STODDERT, Thomas:- Aged (as tis said) Nine-
CC 7   teen Years is by the Court here admitted to
                   Choose his Guardian and hereupon he makes
                   Choice of Benjamin Stoddert of Prince Georges
                   County Gent who in his proper person in Court
                   here declares his willingness to accept the
                   Same-

June 1733   STREET, Francis:- Mary Street widow in her
S 286,287   proper person in Court here binds her Son
                   Francis Street aged Tenn years the 20 day
                   of next February unto George Beall present
                   in Court also until he the said Francis shall
                   arrive to the age of 21 years-Whereupon the
                   said George promises to Learn the said Francis
                   during the term afsd to read & at the Expir-
                   ation thereof to give him a decent Suit of
                   apparel but if the said George Dye before the
                   sd Francis arrive to age then the Contract
                   to be void-

August 1730   STYMPSON, Jeremiah:-(aged as tis said in Court
P 459   here) fifteen years the Eighth day of next

January in his proper person prays the
Justices here that he may be admitted to
choose his Guardian which is granted him
whereupon he makes choice of Peter Hoggins
who upon his declaring in Court here his
willingness to accept the same is admitted
accordingly. On Condition that he the
said Peter Hoggins during this Court do give
Sufficient Security for the said Minors
Estate which he shall receive-

September 1697 SUMERS, male:- Petition of Hannah Edwards,
A 233 "your petitioner having had a child of Sarah
Sumers & bred it up from its infancy as my
own child and as I am informed the said
Sumers Now Sarah Smart unjustly intends to
take this child from me without any consideration, et al., ...Anthony Smart & Sarah
his wife come into court and binds the above
said boy in the above petition Mentioned
unto Archable Edmonson untill 21...he being
11 yeares old the next November to learne
him the trade of a Carpenter...2 Suits of
Cloaths at the Expiration of his Service
of time-

March 1723 L 239,240	TAILOR, William:- Mary Tailor in Court here binds her son William Tailor aged 11 years next February to Rupert Butler or his assigns untill the said William shall arrive to the Age of 21 years and the said Rupert in his proper person in Court here does engage to learn the said William Tailor to read dis- tinctly in the Bible and at the Expiration of his time to give him a decent Suit of Apparell-
June 1726 L 639	TANYHILL, John:- aged (as tis said by his uncle Moses Orme 15 years the 16th day of September last) comes into Court here in his proper person and on his prayer is al- lowed by the Court here to choose his Guard- ian whereupon he makes choice of his said Uncle Moses Orme of this County and the said Moses in his proper person in Court here declaring his willingness to undertake the Guardianship of the said John is by the Court here admitted thereunto-
June 1709 D 173,174	TAYLOR, Ann:- Bethia Taylor came into Court and binds her Daughter Ann Taylor Aged Seven years the Last of January Last past unto William Wattson till age or ye Day of marriage which shall first happen-
November 1727 N 612	TAYLOR, Samuel:- present here in Court in his proper person Six years old the tenth day of October last of the consent of his Mother Mary Taylor present here in Court is by the Court here bound unto the said Allen Lock & Mary his wife until he the said James arrive to

the age of twenty-one years, & hereupon the said Allen Lock in Court here promises to give the said Minor during his time afsd one years Schooling & at the Expiration thereof a Decent Suit of apparel-

August 1746
FF 9
TAYLOR, William:- Son of Thomas and Mary Taylor Aged (as it is said) Seven Months is by the Court here bound to William Price and Anne his Wife until he Arrive to the Age of Twenty one Years and the said William Price and Anne his Wife Engage to give the said William Taylor a Decent Suit of Apparel at the Expiration of his time of Servitude-

September 1699
A 464
THICKPENNY, Hannah:- Aged 2 years old was bound to Thomas Johnson till she arrive to ye age of 16 or day of marriage & in consideration of her being soe young the County is to allow ye said Thomas Johnson one thousand pounds of Tobacco out of the County Leavy-

January 1699
B 15a
THICKPENNY, Henry:- Sonne of John Thickpenny aged 12 years ye 14th of October Last by his ffather was Bound to Major William Barton or his assigns till he arrive to ye age of 21 years-

January 1699
B 15a
THICKPENNY, John:- sone of John Thickpenny Aged 14 years old ye 17th of this Instant by his ffather was bound to Major William Barton or his assignes till he arrives to ye age of 21 years of Age-

January 1699
B 15a
THICKPENNY, Thomas:- Aged 5 years old ye 27th of October Last by his ffather was bound to Daniell Connell or his assigns till

he arrives to be 21 years of age-

November 1721
K 422

THOMAS:- a Bastard Child of Margrett Allen's Aged about Twelve Months is by the Court here Bound unto John Henry & his heirs untill it arrive the age of Twenty one years-

June 1750
LL 176

THOMAS, Gabriel:- Ordered by the Court that Gabriel Thomas Aged about Three months is by the Court here Bound to Philip Mason untill he arrive to the Age of Twenty one years and the said Philip Mason Agrees to give him the freedom Dues according to the Custom of the Country-

August 1747
GG 91

THOMAS, Jesse:- (the son of Catharine Thomas) Aged as tis said Six months and twenty-two days a mulatto is ordered by the Court here to be sold to the highest Bidder and is accordingly Sold for the term prescribed by Act of Assembly to Philip Mason Senr. for the sume of Two thousand one hundred pounds of Tobacco out of which Quantity the said Philip Mason is allowed one Thousand pounds of Tobacco for the trouble he has hitherto been at for keeping and supporting the said Child-

March 1717
H 181

THOMPSON, John:- Son of John Thompson being Nine years old the fourteenth Day of November Last is bound by the consent of the Court to John Howell till he attain his Age according to Act of Assembly the said Howell to learn him to read in the Bible and to give him a new Suit of Apparell at the Expiration of his said time-

June 1706 C 74	TILLY, Ffrancis:- being 4 years old ye first of January Last past, and TILLY, Jane:- two years old ye 4th day of March Last past-, Sone and Daughter to Eliz. Tilly by ye Consent and Choyce of their Mother Bound till age to Timothy Mahoney and his Wife the said Mahoney to give or appoynt them two years Schooleing-
November 1705 B 440	TINNALLY, Phillip:- Servant to Mareen Devall Junior adjudged to be 12 years of age-but ye said Phillip alleadgeing that he had Indentures-Ordered that if he can produce the said Indentures or Sufficient Proofe of ye Same that he serve according to the time Specifyed in the said Indentures, otherwise according to Law-
November 1728 C 334	TIPIN, Anne:- Tenn months old is by the Court here bound to Alexander Falconer until she arrive to age and the said Alexander present here in Court in his proper person promises to learn her to read during the terme afd and at the Expiration thereof to give her a decent suit of apparell and in Consideration of the childs Infancy the said Alexander Falconer is allowed in the present Levey twelve hundred pounds of Tobacco-
November 1744 CC 579	TOMS, Thomas:- is by the Court here admitted to Choose his Guardian and hereupon he makes Choice of George Nicholls of Prince Georges County Planter who in his proper Person in Court here Declares his willingness to accept the Same-

August 1734
V 99

TORFIELD, Thomas:- Hugh Taylor produces to
the Court here Thomas Torfield to be adjudged
of his age who upon Inspection is adjudged
by the Court here to be 15 years an half old-

May 1696
A 11

TUGWELL, Mary:- Ordered that Mary Tugwell
dau of Wm. Tugwell aged four yeares or thereabouts bound out to Thomas Hide according to
Act of Assembly-

March 1725
L 559

TUNNIHILL, John:- aged almost 16 years as its
said by his Aunt Elizabeth Bowen in Court here
moves the Justices hereof that he may be admitted to choose his guardian-he makes Choice
of Leonard Hollyday who declines-

June 1711
G 69

TURKE, James:- Servant to John Norris adjudged
to be 14 years of age ordered to Serve according to Law-

June 1730
P 411

TURNER, John: (Son of the said Mary Turner)
aged five months is by the Court here bound
to James Weems until the said John Arrives
to the age of Twenty one years & the said
James Weems in consideration of the said
Childs tender Infancy is to have Eight hundred pounds of Tobacco in the next County Levy
whereupon the said James promises in open
Court here to learn the said John to read during the term afsd at the Expiration thereof
to give him a decent Suit of apparel-

March 1723
L 239

TURNER, John:- Susannah Turner binds her son
John Turner aged 9 yrs the 29th of this March
Instant to John Norton untill the said boy ar-
rive to the age of 21 years provided the said

John Norton in his proper person in Court here
does ingage to Learn the said John Turner to
Read distinctly in the Bible and at the Expiration of his time to give him a decent suit
of apparel

November 1733   UNGLES, John:- aged as tis said four years
S 473   the ninth day of Last May by the Consent of
                his Mother Mary Ungles present here in Court
                is by the Justices thereof bound unto Robert
                Wall untill the said John shall arrive to
                the age of Twenty years, and the said Robert
                likewise in Court obliges himself to Learn
                the said John during the Term afd to read
                distinctly in the Bible and at the Expir-
                ation thereof to give him a decent Suit of
                apparell-

                            ****

June 1726   VERNALL, Sarah:- Aged at this time about
L 631,632   five years is by the same Justices bound
                to Jonathan Waddams untill age of 16 years-
                said Jonathan is allowed 1200 pds of Tobacco
                in the next County Levy-

August 1722 K 617	WALKER Children:- Ordered by the Court here Thomas Walkers three Children to witt, Elizabeth, Jane & John Walker be delivered to Thomas Gatwood by Paul Bradford, Edward Dyson & Adam Miller with whom they now live it being known to ye Court here that ye said Thomas is runaway & that Rebecca wife of ye sd Tho. Gatwood is Aunt to the said three Children-
March 1739 X 277	WALKER, Mary:- Aged (as tis said) Thirteen years last Febry is by ye Court here Admitted to Chuse her Guardian & thereupon she makes Choice of James Lee of Prince Georges County Planter who in Court here declares his Willingness to Accept ye same-
November 1705 B 439	WALLACE, James:- an Orphan Aged 9 years next March ordered he be with John Anderson till further order and ffurther ordered that is John Hill his ffather in Law doe not appear by the next Court to Shew Cause to ye Contrary that ye said Orphant doe serve ye said Hill or his Assigns till Age-
June 1734 R 89	WARD, Nathan:- Aged (as tis said in Court here) eight years the last day of next February is by Court here bound unto John Swearingen until he the said Nathan shall arrive to the age of Twenty one years Whereupon the said John in his proper person in Court here promises to learn the said Nathan to read during the time afsd & at the expiration thereof to give him a decent Suit of Apparel-
August 1736 W 235	WARING, Basil:- a Minor Aged about Nineteen Years in his proper person prays the Court

here that he may be admitted to Choose his
Guardian Which being Granted him he makes
Choice of his Grandmother Sarah Haddock Who
in Court here Declares her Acceptance thereof-

March 1712 WEATHERBORNE, Peter:- Ordered by the Court
G 175 that Peter Weatherborne Sonn of Jane Weatherborne serve Thomas Plunkett till he attaine
the age of Twenty one years being four months
old the Nineth day of this Moneth-

November 1706 WEBB, Deborah:- Daughter of Humphry Webb aged
C 95a Eight years old bound to Ninian Beall Junior
untill She arrive to age of Sixteen Years-

January 1706 WEBB, Elizabeth:- an Orphant thirteen Years
C 110a of Age bound to Sollomon Rothery till age of
Sixteen or day of Mariage-

November 1706 WEBB, John:- Sonn of Humphry Webb 10 yeares
C 95a of age bound to John Jackson till one and
twenty years of age-

November 1706 WEBB, Mary:- Daughter of Humphrey Webb about
C 96a 5 years of Age Bound to Ishmael Bateman till
age her ffather & Mother both being Runaway-

September 1699 WEBSTER, Ann:- aged nine years old att Christ-
A 464 mas next bound to George Miller till she arrives to ye age of 16 years or ye Day of Mar-
iage-

August 1707 WEBSTER, John:- Servant to Walter Evans ad-
C 154a judged to be 13 Years of Age-Ordered to Serve
the Said Master according to Law-

August 1732 WELCH, Barbara:- Elizabeth Welch in her proper
S 11 person in Court here binds her daughter Barbara
who is 3 years old (as tis said) the 15 of next
October unto William Masters until the said

Barbara comes to age & the said William
Masters in his proper person in Court also
promises to learn her to read during the term
afsd & at Expiration to give her a Decent Suit
of apparel-

March 1742
AA 341

WESTLY, Humphry:- Ordered by the Court here
that Humphry Westly aged about Tenn Months
be bound to Richard King until he arrive to
the Age of Twenty-one Years and the said
Richard King in his Proper Person in Court
here promises to give the said Humphry Westly
a Years Schooling and at the Expiration of
his Time a Decent Suit of Apparel-

August 1721
K 371

WHITE, daughter:- Mary White in Court here
binds her daughter aged about four years
the Twenty fifth day of Aprill next to John
Townly untill it arrive to the age, he thereupon Engages in his proper person in Court
here to Learn her to read distinctly in the
Bible and to give her a decent Suit of Apparel at the Expiration of ye time-

August 1748
HH 341

WHITMORE, John:- an Orphan aged Twelve years
the nineteen day of next January is by the
Court here bound to Humphry Whitmore 'til he
Arrives to the age of Twenty one Years-

November 1708
D 96

WILLETT, Edward:- son of Edward & Tabitha
Willett was born ye 12th of January A.D. 1703
WILLETT, Ninian:- Sonn of Edward & Tabitha
Willett was born ye 30th day of November Ann
Dm 1701
WILLETT, Thomas:- son of Edward & Tabitha
Willett was born ye 9 August 1708-

March 1742 AA 341	WILLIAM:- Captain Thomas Bates Produces to the Court here a Slave named William and desires the Opinion of the Court about the Age of the said Slave and the Justices thereupon adjudge him to be of the Age of fourteen Years-
March 1733 S 248	WILLIAMS, Elizabeth:- Daughter of Jean Williams was born the fourth Day of September 1714 and was Bound to Mary Head Some Small Time after to be with her Untill such Time as your Petitioner should attain or Come to the Age of Sixteen as aforesaid the fourth day of September which was in the year of our Lord 1730-
March 1711 G 43a	WILLIAMS, James:- an Orphant fformerly Liveing with Joshua Hall in his Lifetime bound to Thomas Bell till Age ye Said Bell obleidging himselfe to keep him to his Learning-
March 1722 K 486	WILLIAMS, Jeremiah:- Jeremiah Williams in his person in Court here binds his son named Jeremiah Williams aged four years the Eighteenth day of May next to Robert Oram & his Wife untill ye sd Boy arrive to ye age of Twenty-one years he ye sd Robert here oblidging himselfe to Learn ye boy to read distinctly and at ye Expiration of his Time to give him a decent Suit of Apparel-
March 1729 O 411	WILLIAMS, Henry:- a poor Orphan Child Aged (as tis said) three months the twenty-fifth of this Instant March is by the Court here bound unto Nehemiah Ogden blacksmith until it shall arrive to Age and the said Nehemiah present here in Court in his proper person

promises to Learn the said Orphan during the
term to read and write as likewise to bring
him up to the art and mystery of a blacksmith
and at the Expiration of his time to give him
a decent Suit of Apparell and the said Nehemiah in Consideration of the Childs Infancy
is to be allowed one thousand pounds of Tobacco in the next County Levy-

March 1729
O 411

WILLIAMS, John:- a poor Orphan boy aged (as
tis said) three Years or thereabouts is by
the Court here bound unto Nehemiah Ogden
blacksmith until it shall arrive to Age and
the said Nehemiah present here in Court in
his Proper Person promises to Learn the said
Orphan during the term to read and write as
likewise to bring him up to the art and Mystery of a blacksmith and at the Expiration of
his time to give him a decent Suit of Apparell-

November 1729
P 272

WILLIAMS, Mary:- dau of Baruch Williams Aged
twelve years as tis said is admitted in her
proper person in Court here to choose her
Guardian and accordingly makes Choice of the
reverend Mr. Murdock who likewise in Court
here accepts the guardianship and it is ordered by the Court here the afsd Guardian give
security at March Court next for the said
Marys Estate-

March 1717
H 182

WILLIAMS, William:- Son of James and Sarah
Williams is by Consent of the Court bound to
Nathaniel Wickham and Sabina his Wife till
he arrive to Age According to Act of Assembly
being five years old the fifth of January last

and he the said Nathaniel Wickham and Sabina
his Wife or either of them to give him a new
Suit of Apparrell at the Expiration of his
time-

November 1717
H 310

WILLIAMS, William:- an Orphan bound to
Ruport Butler and Ann his now Wife till the
said William comes to age according to Act
of Assembly...he being now Seven Years Old-

March 1722
K 486

WILLIAMS, Willm:- Jeremiah Williams in his
proper person in Court here also binds his
Son Willm Williams aged nine Years the Twenty
Second day of August next to Charles Drury &
his Wife untill ye sd Wm. arrive to ye age
of Twenty one Years he ye sd Charles here
oblidging himself to Learn ye boy to read
distinctly & write a Legible hand & at ye
Expiration of his time to give him a decent
Suit of Apparrell as also pay unto Robert
Oram one hundred & fifty pounds of Tobacco-

March 1711
G 43

WILLSON, William:- Son in Law to William Hill
Deceased aged 15 years of Age-came into Court
and was bound to James Nuttwell till Age ye
Said James obleidgeing himselfe to give him
a years Schooleing-

November 1736
W 263

WILSON, Henry:- aged as Tis Said in Court
here Fifteen Years next January is by the
Justices thereof Admitted to Choose his Guardian Whereupon he makes Choice of Osborn Sprigg
of the County afsd Gent Who in his proper person in Court here Declares his Willingness to
Accept the Same-

November 1724
L 380

WILSON, Joseph:- of a Competent Age as tis
said) comes into Court here in his proper

person and on his motion is allowed by the
Court here to choose his Guardian, whereupon
his brother Lingan Wilson of the County afd,
and the said Lingan in Court here declaring
his willingness to undertake the Guardianship
of his said brother is by the Justices here
Admitted thereunto-

August 1727
N 490

WILSON, Joshua:- (son of Major Josiah Wilson
deced) aged against as tis said fifteen years
or thereabouts comes into Court here & on his
prayer is allowed by the Justices thereof to
choose his Guardian whereupon he makes choice
of his Brother Lingan Wilson & the said Lingan
in his proper person in Court here declaring
his willingness to undertake the Guardianship
of the said Joshua is by the Court here admitted thereunto-

June 1718
H 671

WILSON, Josiah:- Josiah Wilson comes into
open Court and chuses Mr. Daniel Dulany his
Guardian who is admitted accordingly-

June 1719
H 861

WILSON, Lingan:- Came into open Court and
Prayed that Mr. Joseph Belt might be admitted
his Guardian which is ordered accordingly-

August 1728
O 245

WILSON, Martha:- Ordered by the Court here
that Elizabeth Wilson (guardian to her Sister-
in Law Martha Wilson, daughter of Major Josias
Wilson deced) bring her said Ward to this Court
during the present Sessions or that she give
Security for the said Orphans Estate being per-
fectly delivered her when of full age according
to which order afterwards the said Martha aged
(as tis said) about fifteen Years Came into

116

Court here in her proper person and prayed
She might be admitted to Choose her guardian
anew which is granted-Whereupon she made
Choice of her Brother Lingan Wilson who upon
declaring in Court here his Willingness to
accept the Same is admitted Accordingly-

August 1745
DD 178

WITHERS, Rebecca:- Aged (as tis said) Three
Years in June last (with the Consent of her
Mother Mary Wood) is by the Court here bound
unto Richard and Jane King until she Arrive
to the Age of Sixteen Years and the said
Kings Promise during the Term aforesaid to
give the said Rebecca one years Schooling and
at the Expiration of her Time of Servitude
to give her a Decent Suit of Apparel-

November 1703
B 262a

WORMWOOD, William:- Servt to Mr. Clement Hill
adjudged sixteen years of Age-ordered thereupon ye said Wormedwood Serve Mr. Clem^t Hill
or his Assignes according to an Act of Assembly in Such Cases made and provided-

June 1733
S 287

YOUNG, Jacob:- Two years old Last March is
by the Court here bound unto Philip Plasay
untill he the said Jacob shall arrive to
the age of Twenty-one years Whereupon the
said Philip in his proper person in Court
promises to Learn the said Jacob during the
Term afd to Read and at the Expiration thereof to give him a decent Suit of apparel-

INDEX

i

vii